ARRIVAL PRESS

STRAIGHT FROM THE HEART

Edited

By

TRUDI RAMM

First published in Great Britain in 1993 by
ARRIVAL PRESS
1 - 2 Wainman Road, Woodston,
Peterborough, PE2 7BU

Foreword

I remember my first ever love poem. I cringe to think about it now as it was sent to a teacher that I had a huge crush on in my secondary school. I remember walking into his classroom, for my next lesson, whilst he was reading it. I was unable to concentrate for the rest of the week through sheer embarrassment! However, I have had more luck with my scribblings since and I find it one of the best ways of getting my feelings known.

The poets included in this collection have poured out their feelings into one of the best anthologies that I have had the honour of editing. Each poem, some to a love lost and some to a loved one, is full of feeling and comes straight from the heart.

Whether you are in love or looking for love I am sure that this book will bring out the old romantic in you and that each poem will take on a special meaning for you, as they did for me.

Trudi Ramm
Editor

Contents

Your Love and Mine

The warmth, the security of
  love in your heart,
The love which you keep
  the love you impart,
Only people in love know
  the tenderness there,
The tenderness of having
  someone to care.

The love that no man
  can tear apart,
The love that is rooted
  deep in your heart,
The love never ending
  the love always true,
The love that means life
  for me and for you.

Carole Watson

Maybe

Maybe if I wish upon a star
Our new love will go far.
Maybe if I say a prayer tonight
Everything will work out alright.
Maybe if I tell you *I Love You*
You'll say you love me too.
Maybe my searching is over at last
And heartbreak will be a thing of the past.

Christine Coupe

Door to Love

Betty Sims you are wonderful,
You are so caring and giving.
I thank Father God every day in prayer
For a jewel so radiant and beyond compare,
Also that He made you mine.
You are a handsome woman
and so gently kind and fine.
You kicked out the strife
And made, for us together, a wonderful life
For you and me my generous wife.
You are so lovely that I want to say
That when I met you sweetheart
My happiness in life really made a start,
Replacing the pain and the worry before.
To love, life and laughter
You flung wide open the door.

Kevin E Sims

Loving You

How easy to say *I Love You* standing hand in hand
In church beneath the alter to join this woman and this man
For richer or for poorer means not financial wealth
But security and happiness, an abundance of good health.
For better or for worse, is hard to understand
When things are going very wrong
Not quiet the way we planned.
Mistakes are often made
Some bitter cruel remarks
The loss of trust and loving
Where did we lose our track?
It's easy to say sorry
But harder to forgive
But hold on very tightly
I'm sure our love could live
Just give the chance of loving
Let the healer lend a hand
For time is on our side Dear
Join back this woman and this man.

Wilma MacLellan

What is Love?

Love is romantic and radiant
Ecstatic and fun.
It's sensational and emotional,
Warm like the sun.

Love grows like a flower,
Untamed and carefree.
It is charming and golden
And joyful to see.

It's like flying in heaven,
Paradise without wings.
Happiness and fulfilment
Is what love brings.

Sally-Anne Young

A Love Without You

I can't imagine another love,
Not without my one and only, you.
I just love all the good, bad things that you do.
Please let's make another go of things.
Then from there together, see what the future brings.
I love most of all your smile, the way you touch.
I just can't get enough of those things
As I love them all very much.
When we fight and you push me away
Sometimes I get frightened that's where I'll stay.
I don't want to lose you really I don't,
So promise me you won't push me away,
Please promise you won't.
I love you my darling
Take care, God bless.

Rachael Smith

My Love

You my love are everything to me,
and no matter what this will always be,
I've given you the key, the key to my heart,
and you will have this even if we part.

When I'm sad and need a friend,
I turn to you and my troubles end,
You make me laugh, you make me cry,
Still all together you're a wonderful guy.

You've given me a priceless love
You must be a gift from God above,
They say love is blind, and maybe this is true,
but all I want to say is that
I love you.

Susan Kent

Sharing

To share in pleasures of the flesh,
Conceived by some as sin,
By people who will never know,
Of breaking mental barriers,
Allowing dreams to flow.

Wrapped in strong supporting arms,
Hot breath on lightly scented skin,
Embracing each selfless motion,
Revelling in the freedom,
Each tender moment brings.

Scorned by others racked with jealousy,
Turned by bitter minds, the collective social,
Conscious screams sordid promiscuity,
Regardless of such ignorance,
The pleasure is mine to give.

It brings to mind such sadness,
That some could not begin,
To understand the special untainted friendship,
That comes only from within.

Denise McCarthy

Loving

Your hand holding mine
Your soft gentle touch,
The smile in your eyes
That means so much.
The special jokes
That only we share,
The way you hold me
And the way you care.
Plans for the future
We often make
Friendship we've found
That will never break.
Those three little words
So simple and true,
As you kiss me gently
And say *I love you*!

Suzanne N Bowen

'Til you Return

Hi! Just a note to say hello.
A little message to let you know,
How much I love and miss you so,
I wish you'd never had to go.

You're never far away from mind.
Because to me, you are so kind,
I'll have to love and leave you now,
But you'll always be in my thoughts somehow.

Wendy R Dawson

In Love

The moon is shining up above and
Down below we're so much in love.
My eyes meet yours and then we kiss
And in my mind the world around us
Just doesn't exist.

Kelly Gough

Heartache

Do you remember the day you left me?
All I could do was cry
I thought my heart would surely break,
I wished that I could die,
I waited for weeks just to hear your voice
A sound that never came.
I made so many new promises
But all that too was in vain.
I loved you oh so very much,
I longed for your smile or your slightest touch,
Now as I think of you again,
The memories, your face all I feel is pain.
I think of the night you said goodbye,
And quietly again I begin to cry.

Terri O'Connor

Love Match

Your eyes are blue and mine are grey,
You're broad and I am slight,
And yet our wordless language
Says the same, night after night.

You like to read, I love to dance.
You go, I wait and see.
But when it comes to feelings,
We're true soulmates, you and me.

We tease, we trust, we talk 'til dawn,
Solemn or mad as loons.
Then sleep in morning harmony,
All smiles and curled like spoons.

Our differences are paltry,
We're devoted, man and wife
Sharing hopes and fears and kisses
And a love that lasts for life.

Carol Anne Davis

Remember Me

Summertime is here again,
remember me, remember when . . .
Remember the nights down by the sea
I loved you and you loved me.

Remember the days, hand in hand
we would go down the beach, making love hearts in the sand.
Remember the days together we'd drive
go anywhere, anyplace I felt so alive.

Now the summertime has come back again
Please remember me and remember when . . .

Tammy Fudgell

Long Night

Hours linger
seeming endless
darker forever darker
moods of depression
sadden my heart
as It thinks
only of you
and of our brighter
days and times together
such a long night
thinking not sleeping
dawn breaking
birds singing
with their mocking call
with no apparent reason
only in that they have awoken
In harmony together
I wish we could be
that way again
Together
after the long night.

Myk Jonson

Ocean Love

To stand before a quiet shore
Reflects a distant soul
Where deep inside the river cries
A heart that someone stole
To smile upon a memory
Horizons melt unto the sea
Where once a love was running free
No time to care for what may be
To look upon a face with love
And smile
Lost tidings never gone for good
For what has passed has been and only could
Be remembered, loved and cherished all the while.

Michelle Blaiberg

Valentine

Valentine's Day, no cards in the post,
No bottle of wine, no love to toast,
an empty room, a lonely heart,
Never forgetting when we had to part,
No *I love you* on Valentine's Day,
No tender kisses to come my way,
Then a drink in the pub, valentines galore,
You sang our song, then we both knew the score,
Both holding hands, in silence we kissed,
Realising that each other we missed,
Then you said *I love you* I wish you were mine,
And together we said *be my Valentine*
A long time had lapsed since we had to part,
But each of us held, a piece of each other's heart,
Then tonight you held me, it's been such a long time,
And you made up my day,
when you said,
I love you
Be my Valentine.

Janet Simnor

Love Another Day

Love, they say, can conquer all.
Some succeed, but others fall,
along the way,
but live to love another day.
What is life without love?
Everyone has needs.
Physical attraction . . .
. . . or just kindly deeds.
So if you've loved
and fallen by the way,
get up and
live to love another day.

Mavis Fox

Unforgettable

His voice is a wave of emotion,
his smile is a bird in a storm,
his face is a maze undiscovered,
in his mind is a star to be born.

The tears which he sheds without crying,
the embrace which he gives without touch,
the look in his eyes without seeing,
are all of them things which I love.

The warmth of his arms when he holds me,
the soft breath which falls on my cheek,
the love which he gave me so freely,
all memories I'm going to keep.

Alexandra Haigh

Waiting for You

The shore looks empty without you here
Making love on the sand and having you near
Remember how we met and I first caught your eye
From that moment on our love was destined to never die.

I remember thinking it could never be
I thought you were too good for a girl like me
With your beautiful face and personality the same
But you saw beauty inside, our love was not just a game.

But then oh remember that terrible day
Fresh tears are falling oh why did I say
That our love was to perfect it couldn't last
And that you'd leave me and I'd become a face of the past.

Oh my torment is great I sealed your fate
Those words were an omen but now it's too late
Your body perhaps lies out in the sea
And if that is true it's because of me.

If you're gone, rest in peace where happiness you found
Oh how we used to love the ocean its sound
I'll never stop hoping you'll come back not I
Until your body they find I'm not saying goodbye.

Sharon Miller

What is Love

Love, now that's a thing,
A friendly smile, a way of knowing.
A tender touch, that happiness can bring.
Love is waiting, love is wanting.
Love is never having to say you're sorry.
Love is always being there.
Love is sharing, love is caring,
How the other one may feel.
But I know little of this thing called Love.
Love walked out one cold dark night,
Love left me alone, love left me bitter,
Love left me sad.
Love left me to cry alone,
Loved changed from good to bad.
Love can be so gentle,
Love can be so cruel
Love can turn to hatred.
Love can be a fool.

E M Drabble

Love Hurts

I sit alone and watch the raindrops
Every one a single tear
I think of him with another girl
I look at me just sitting here.

I look again the rain has stopped
The clouds begin to part
I know now our love has gone
Although he's broken my heart

I must forget him, I say to myself
My friends all say the same
I wipe away one final tear
Now I know love's only a game

Jacky Cole

Regretting

I've seen another side of you,
Seen beneath the hide of you,
And I'm not sure I'm liking what I see,
We all have another side
Many things we try to hide,
It's bringing out another side of me.
Can we be
Regretting, some of us waste our time regretting
And forgetting that we've been that way before,
Those of us who never learn
Reach out fingers that still burn
To play that same old half remembered score.
Regretting, the giving and getting
That should be part of every love affair,
And now I've wakened up to see
That all the giving came from me,
Regretting, one more time, for you don't care.

Angie Von Tobel

Holiday Romance

Every time I think about you
I cannot help, but cry
You left me on the camp, alone
You didn't say *goodbye.*
I asked you to come and see me
I thought your love was true
But you left me there without you
And left me feeling blue.
I only have the card you wrote
You posted through the door
I opened it, to read inside
I love you, ever more
The tears began to trickle down
I wanted my love here
I hope that I'll see you again
I hope I will next year.
But until then, I'll have to dream
And hope that pain will heal
I'll dream of you until the end
And hope our love was real.

Dianne Wolfenden

Forever

The love you gave me
Made me whole
You caressed my body
And touched my soul
The strength passed from you
And entered in
Like a sweet young blossom
It flowered within
Our hearts entwined
And soared so high
A thousand stars burst forth
In a rich blue sky
Lost deep in a passion
A heady perfume
So strong and potent
Like a honeysuckle bloom
Reaching the heights of ecstasy
We drank deep of the wine
Our love was sealed
Forever in time.

Ann C Thomas

Silver Wedding

I close my eyes, then sink back into time
To a church filled with people, to love in its prime.
Here is a couple, with faces aglow,
With eyes for no other, hearts beating low.

Could nobody tell me, nobody say,
That life will just last for a year and a day?
If they only had spoken, only had said,
Hold on to the minutes, for soon they are fled.

But life will go by, life will not stay,
Though you bind it with love, it will still slip away;
Though you stitch it with teardrops, wrung from your heart
The minutes will still speed away and depart:

If I open my eyes, what now shall I see?
Why, the same burning love is still holding me.
Each beat of the heart, each wondering breath
Just strengthens the bond that transcends even Death.

For it's part of a pattern, part of a plan,
The meaning of which is a mystery to man.
The weaver of time holds us all in his hand,
Not yet, 'til the crossing, shall we understand.

Shirley Frances Winskill

My Love

When my eyes first met yours, of emerald green,
They were the most beautiful eyes, I have ever seen,
I never thought, that we would get together,
But it feels like, we have been together forever,
All I ever wanted, was to hold you in my arms,
And smother you, with all my charms,
I always said you were the best,
Truly kind not like the rest,
Now I can look at you, every single night,
Just to make sure, you're safe and tight,
My darling I love you, with all my heart,
Let's hope our love, will never part.
My life would not be the same, without you,
So when you die, my love will follow too.
You will not have to wait that late,
I will meet you outside, those pearly gates.

Eamonn Costello

Bequest

Deep in a mood of solemn thought,
To me this life was chiefly taught,
A thing apart maybe, 'tis more,
Of this my love I'm surely sure,
Of all my blessings ere bestowed,
'Tis you above all who canst behold,
A wealth of love within your reach,
A bounding heart, 'tis yours to teach,
Of dreams galore, of fancies few,
It's yours this heart, bequest to you.

G E Smith

Devotion

With years of patience and devotion
Seeming as without emotion;

The careless word so oft' endured;
To thoughtless wit and jibes inured

Is rarely seen the hurt's embrace
In the bright eyes of a loving face.

Ted Herbert

Tears

When did the loving stop?
When did the hate creep in?
How could the love we had, commit its greatest sin?
It only took a moment to wipe away the years
And leave the broken pieces drowning in my tears.
One moment you were there, the next you had gone
Then I faced a night time my whole life long
Were you in her arms, as we always used to be?
When the two of us together, lived so happily
We made the plans of sweethearts with every sweet caress
I didn't stop to think, whilst in my happiness
There'd be some day you'd tire and leave me on one side
Taking another in my place to be your loving bride.
Don't stay away too long my love, the pain is so severe
When she discards you for another, then I shall still be here.

Patricia Taylor

Love Nest

Love is like a bird in the palm of my hand,
Nourish it well, for it to grow and be grand.
Love I'll cherish and never let go,
Cradle it gently not to hurt it so.
May it always feel my gentle clasp,
Love is food to enjoy giving energy that lasts.
I hear it sing, striking chords in my heart,
One day my hand will be forced apart.
Leaving it empty here on my palm,
Love is so sacred may it never come to harm.

Gloria M Rees

Untitled

Love, love, love,
What's your call,
Stead, with strings,
Of friendship, that's all,

Fun, fun, fun,
Where's your line,
Interests you enjoy,
Most essential, are mine.

M Turner

Besotted

(dedicated to Emma Jane Williams)

The purity of my lady doth inspire
Repressive thoughts of desire.
In mine eyes thou art perfection,
Beauty of a merest reflection.
A pose in rapture - an artist's capture.

Lost in an adoring gaze,
My pounding heart betrays
Fears of a reject dealt,
by Cupid's cruel arrow felt.

As devotion's flames are fanned,
Waiting in anonymity
is a fool romancing a fair maiden's hand,
Wanting in courage
to make an impassioned stand.

She doth arouse a dilemma -
Sacred love or the scorn of Emma?
A cloud of her sweet scent
and I'm no longer able to repent.

Admiration of her slightest motion,
A captive of love's unique potion.
Emma, thou hast claimed my heart,
Never shall my love depart.

Woodward

Loser in the End

What is this hate you're feeling
what makes you seem so blue?
It does no good to linger
on wrongs befallen you.

Your life has come so twisted,
your heart so full of hate,
you must forgive, you must forget.
before it is too late.

Why waste your years on yearning
for love you'll never gain.
he's gone, let go, farewell,
to all his hurt and pain.

Pick up the threads of your life,
learn to smile again.
Throw off your veil of sadness
or be a loser in the end.

Carol Lynne

Love - My Heart

Here is my heart,
It's yours take it,
Do what you will
Please don't break it.
Here are my arms
To hold you tight
Keep you safe,
Through the night.
Here are my eyes
To convert you with,
To see a vision
My woman,
I love with.
To see you,
From deep within.
My heart and soul,
Is that a sin?
To love.
And be loved.
That's my desire!
Come with me,
Light my fire.

Rayo M Tucker

Lost Love

The days are long, the nights are too
I am full of love, but where are you?
You left me in my twilight years
For me to realise all my fears
To be left alone in later life
In a world that is full of hate and strife
Despair and anguish tears me apart
Because I no longer have a place in your heart

So when you start down your new road
I want you to know the burden and load
That I will take with me to the grave
Because of the love you said I never gave
The love that is here and locked inside
The love I tried so hard to hide
I must try and start to live again
But I don't know how and I don't know when
The chances are the time will be long
And I will just go on thinking where things went wrong

Why was I the last to know how you really felt
Before that fateful card was dealt
We could have really tried and tried
To release the love that was locked inside
But the die is cast and the deed is done
The battle is fought - I have lost - she has won!

Anne Ratcliffe

Love Story

I would write a story of a love so fond and true,
A story that begins and ends about my love for you;
Of the days that seem so empty when you are not near
And yet so full of happiness, when you my love are here.
Why are the days so long my love when you are far away?
And when I see you dearest love, I wish that you could stay.

The minutes fly, the hours fly, why do you have to go?
I wonder if it is because I really love you so.
We've set the date, our new life to begin, and soon the time
When I, my dearest, will be yours and you'll be mine,
But the story is not finished, 'til we go hand in hand,
And really show each other life's glorious promised land.

Vera Hansson

Love Letters

You sent me letters every day
When we were young and far apart
Letters of love, from you my dear
I kept them close to my heart.

Posted overseas, but your memories
I cherished for ever more
Your corny little quips, kept your stiff upper lip
As you bravely fought the war.

Your careful hand chose words so true
Each line was touched with tenderness
And hopes and dreams we planned to share
A lifetime of togetherness.

As the years flew by, my bundle has grown
The ribbons now faded, the ink is less blue
Sadly you are no longer here
But I still have something to remind me of you.

Katherine Delaney

The Broken Heart

I am so sad and
a little distressed
in fact too much
to bother to dress

My heart is broken
because of you
my mind's in a turmoil
what can I do

You've treated me badly
it's so hard to believe
do you think
I was out to deceive

You, yes you
to whom I would do no harm
just for a little love
I would have given an arm.

Where to now
for each of us
do we say goodbye
without any fuss.

Tom Sullivan

I Care

I have my life, my time, my space
The spring, the air, your pretty face
I have no right to plan next week
It's only peace each day I seek

I stop, I look, I talk with pride
My love for life - no wish to hide
The silver lining's always there
I write, I hope, I love, I care

Raymond Brown

Primrose Hill

I met a girl out on a hill
And saw that she was weeping
I thought that I should pass her by
But my heart went to her fleeting
And as I passed I caught her gaze
A look which mesmerised me
Within her eyes she seemed to hold
A thousand broken visions
And though I would reach out to her
I could not ease her sorrow
For suddenly she slipped away
She was a fleeting shadow

Lucy Halahan

First Date

Mum I'm in such a hurry
I haven't got much time
please will you iron this dress for me
and give my shoes a shine.

I haven't wrapped this present yet
Mum can I borrow your pen
do you think Dad will let me stay
at least until half ten.

Oh no, my hair won't curl.
Will you tie this bow for me
if I cover this spot with make-up
will anybody see.

It's half past eight already
I don't think he's going to come
say he doesn't like me now
and takes someone else, oh Mum.

Oh here he is at last
do I look alright to you
No I don't look like a princess
and Mum, I love you too.

Josephine Nuttall

My Personal Alphabet

A is for my lover's name
B for what we share - the blame
C is for what cannot be Denied and that's my *love for thee.*
Everyday we have to wait,
Forbidden love must hesitate.
Golden are the days we've had
Hearts united made us glad.
I love you and that's for sure.
Joyous days we'll find once more.
K for kisses that we shared -
L for love - if we just dared.
Music, magic in my life,
Never though to be your wife.
Oh to be together though,
Perhaps, one day, we'll make it so.
Quiet the days you are not here
Relief I feel when you appear.
Sugar and sweetness, sharpness and sour,
Trouble and turbulence beyond our power.
Upset by things that we must do,
Vows we made both me and you.
Wedding rings, both yours and mine,
Xtramarital is not our line.
You and I our lives must mend.
Z's the finish - Z's the end.

Margaret Williams

Everlasting Love

You are my man
You are my life
I am so glad darling
that you made me your wife
your love is true
your love is bliss
remember darling our very first kiss

Several years have passed us by
I know our love will never die
So my love these words I say
I'll love you 'til my dying day

M Roberts

Danny

I waited such a long time
Just to see your face
Now I see you always
In my heart you hold a place

I watch you every minute
At home, at work and play
I love you every second
Of each and every day

I couldn't ask for a better love
You are precious like pure gold
I love you so much Danny
My son, of six years old.

Chris West

Together

Together we are. Together we'll stay.
We'll love each other 'til the end of our days.
My feelings for you are way up the line.
You're kind, and considerate, that suits me just fine.
You say that you love me, you're part of my dreams.
I'm floating on clouds well that's how it seems.
The times we are together, it all feels so right,
I just want to kiss you and hold you so tight,
I know it's forever you won't go away.
Together we are. Together we'll stay.

Mandy Penn

Your Eyes

Your eyes are of a turquoise pale,
not deep and rich like sea or vale,
but just one glance and they capture me,
'til a field of jewels I'd no longer see,
or cream puff clouds with a custard sun,
it is still your eyes which I cannot shun.
On nature's glories our eyes should feast,
but on nature's banquet I gorge the least.
Your eyes they fill me to the brim
and leave me weak from limb to limb.
I cannot fight their passionate plea,
or silence the words they speak to me.
Your eyes, they draw me to your heart,
at once I'm whole, no longer part.
While all around us nature dances,
she asks no questions, seeks no answers.
Her beauty boasts her every scene.
She holds the key to every dream,
but still I'm blinkered to it all
and for your eyes alone, I fall.

Sara Williams

One Kiss

One kiss before we say goodnight
Is all I ask of you.
You are my heavenly delight.
Your eyes, flame blue,
Enrich my inner vision bright.

How shall I describe your hair?
I can only say
Its darkness is to me more fair
Than the brightest day.

Why tell you what is in my heart,
You ask - why lay it bare,
When any moment we must part?

My dearest man, I only dare
To speak, because I know it's true
That I love you.

Dorothy Campbell

To Love Him

To love is to know him
That's what they say
But do I love him
Do I know him
My heart asks me each day

I think I love him
I think I know him
But deep down I'm not sure
Because do I love him
Do I know him
I know not once more

S J Cooke

Constancy

When I was seventeen I fell in love,
His voice was gentle as a turtle dove,
Lustrous eyes which gazed and gazed on me
Were bluer than the deepest azure sea.

Fair curly hair adorned his fresh young brow,
If I but close my eyes I see it now.
He smiled the smile that stole my heart away
And made me vow I'd ever with him stay.

We married on a day in early spring,
He on my wedding finger placed a ring.
A band of gold which then bound him to me,
This cord of love until eternity.

His brow is furrowed now, his face grows old,
Yet still there's silver curls where once was gold.
Our lives have mellowed as the years pass by.
But I will love him 'til the day I die.

Margaret Aitken

To My Man

As I glance up at the clear blue sky,
A single tear slowly falls from my eye,
I'm missing you more than words can say,
And I cry for you each and every day.
Because now I know you are the one and only guy for me,
I still talk to you, even though you're gone.
Because I know our hearts beat as one.
I love you from the bottom of my heart,
And always think of you, even though we're apart,
So just reach out your hand and I'll be there,
Showing you how much I really do care.
I will take you in my arms and hold you tight,
And I'll make sure together we'll be alright,
I will let you laugh and I will let you cry,
But I'll never let you say goodbye.
And with all my love I'll send you my heart,
Hoping and praying we never again will part,
My happiness now lies on us soon being back together,
When we can then be with each other forever,
But until that day arrives for us to see,
Please save all your thoughts and love for me.

J Alenson

The Fallen Star

I loved so long, but long ago, and loved you more each day.
I thought you'd never leave my side, but *love is blind* they say.
For I was wrong, and when you left, I knew I too must go,
But I remember of our love in heat of winter's snow.

I know someday you will return when sky falls to the ground,
When happiness dispels all pain, and tears no more are found.
I long to hold you just once more; your memory grips my heart,
But years have passed since we last met - that day we chose to part.

O restless heart and foolish mind, I scorn you, yet alas,
You're all I had through these long years which took so long to pass,
But now I'm back - those wasted years but gave my heart fresh hope,
That you would take me in your arms and love me as before.

There's nothing here I recognise; no people whom I know,
I can't pretend now anymore; my dreams died long ago.
I never held you, or your love, for someone else held that.
'Twas all a dream - a silent lie, I cherished in my heart.

Linda Walker

Perfect Dream

By the water fountain,
That glistens in the sun,
Beside the tallest mountain
That's where my dreams begun.

For at that precious moment,
When earth and time stood still,
You asked me if I'd marry you
and I replied, 'I will.'

We parted then reluctantly
as day turned into night,
But met again so happily
In morning fresh sunlight.

We hugged and kissed, and danced and sang
so merrily together,
For it was then I realised
I wanted you forever.

But then it happened the truth came back
as I awoke to find,
That dreams are dreams and always will
be happenings in the mind.

Deborah Confrey

Emotion

You've never seen like this, don't understand it at all
You thought I'd crumble after such a bad fall.
I can't let it happen must be stronger than that.
So I speak without feeling my voice empty and flat.
My heart keeping the real me inside
Is the only the place where I can hide
All the pain and tears I can't let out
As I silently scream for the one I'm nothing without.
You'll never know what you've done to me.
It's hidden in the hope you'll never see
Hidden with a burning love for you.
Even after what you've put me through
It will always burn there, that won't change
Living apart will forever seem strange.
I could easily forgive you if you'd only come back
Could even teach the respect your loving lacks
Your love could silence my pain and commotion
Setting my heart free to feel emotion.

Helen Rafferty

From Me to You

I've never had this feeling,
The one I get when I'm with you.
A feeling of completeness,
Togetherness it's true.
For you have made me realise,
What life can offer me.
And you've shown me all the best things,
In life are always free.
Whenever you are with me,
Whenever you're around.
I feel so very lucky,
For this happiness I've found.
I've fallen for you deeply,
It's possible to be.
That all this time I never thought,
You could belong to me.

Lisa Starr

True Love

If you should ever leave me
How would my life go
Not so far, believe me
Because I love you so.

My life is wrapped around you,
With you I'm so complete
Love and devotion surround you
Each morning as we greet.

Every minute of every day
You are in my thoughts and mind
Every hour in every way
Some added pleasures I find.

Irene Duggleby

Dream Girl

Untouched by any human hand,
More virgin than the driven snow,
The fairest maid in any land,
Both tender and so nice to know.

Her gentle features, lovely hair,
Inviting smile that's so unique,
The love and warmth she wants to share,
So cool, sincere, with such mystique.

She creeps into my dreams at night,
And quick departs at early dawn,
For her all evil I would fight,
Delilah, she my hair could shorn.

Her heart beats soft, affectedly,
She's full of ardour, full of zeal,
My love for her runs readily,
Is more than passion, more than real.

And when I close my eyes at night,
She starts to set my mind a-whirl,
I know she's only in my sight,
My own, my own, my own dream girl!

S Mason

Partnership

You've brought me sincerity, understanding and caring,
The importance of trust, the pleasure of sharing,
The meaning of love, shown by kindness and passion,
These you give gladly, ignoring the fashion.

My love is exciting, brings a purpose to living,
Your love is protective, yet intense in its giving,
Obsessed by emotion essential in lovers,
Our pleasures are mutual, fulfilment discovers.

I cherish our future, upholding each vow,
A life-long commitment . . . as time will allow.

Rosalie Langham

Straight From the Heart

The first time we met
I knew I wanted you
and when you took me in your arms
it was like a dream come true.

I hated being away from you
when we had to part
because somewhere along the way
you stole away my heart.

I remember the hazy summer days
and the precious times we shared
special moments in my heart
that proved how much I cared.

You've brought me more than happiness
I need you more each day
you're a very special person
I love you more than words can say.

Catherine Ward

When You Walked Into My Cafe . . .

You moved towards the counter, my toes began to curl,
As you asked me for a cup of tea and a chocolate viennese whirl.
My hand began to tremble as I passed the cup of tea,
When our hands touched the sudden excitement was like a
surge of electricity.
'Iced bun and a coffee luv,' I heard a customer shout.
It brought me back to earth as if I'd landed with a clout.
And then to my surprise, you asked me for a date,
I replied yes so quickly, I daren't hesitate.
The date was arranged before you had to go
The exciting anticipation left me with a rosy glow.
Since that day many things have happened between us.
We were definitely blessed by the god of love Venus.
When you walked into my cafe, you walked into my life.
I knew we'd make a perfect couple, now I am your wife.

Jodie Upton

To My Valentine

This little note dear Valentine
Is addressed to you -
It's to say -
I love you -
Love you through and
Through.
And as today is a special
Day - for those in love like
Us -
I'm sending extra rays of Love -
To join the two of us.

Meryl Tookaram

My Wife

The love of my life
You are my wife
With your eyes so blue
And a heart that's true
You're a mother a lover a housewife as well
I love you so much that I just want to tell
The world that it's great to have a woman like you
To love me and care for me and our son too
And when I am down and need picking up
You give me a smile and a warm loving cup
Of kindness and cuddles and good things in life
You are my true love forever my wife.

P Dolby

Love

I don't think that I can see
A better place I'd like to be
Than with you every night and day
And there I know I'd love to stay
For though we may be far apart
Our love grows here deep in my heart
through good and bad and thick and thin
I know together we can win.

S Box

Is it Love?

Is it electric lightning?
A bolt out of the blue?
Is it a flame - a burning fire?
Or just a spark that grew?
Is it a shooting star now?
Exploded in the sky.
Is it a snowflake on the ledge?
A song that makes you cry?
Is it a smile each morning?
Or kisses in the rain?
Is it the shaking warm sensation when you hear his name?
Is it the waves just crashing,
Down on the sandy shore?
Is it the sunset in the sky
You've never seen before?
Is it the glint of golden
Sent from the moon above?
Is it a feeling - felt to be believed in -
Is it love?

Julie Boorman

Him

Curled up in my bed, it's impossible to sleep,
Awake in my thoughts, are the memories I keep
Of the day that I met him and the joy that I've had,
Makes my reason for living, a time to be glad.

The feelings I have were not there from the start,
But little by little they've captured my heart,
And now it's too late to turn back the time
For all that I want, is him to be mine.

With lingering touches, like feathers on skin,
And my emotional thoughts - where can I begin?
To describe what it's like with him by my side
Is leaving my defences open wide.

He was right, when he said that it could be fun,
To hold and to cuddle and so become one;
Now the magical mystery tour's on its way,
Let's forget about tomorrow and live for today.

Glenn Lee

Untitled

Baby, I won't cry
If you don't go away
I really won't cry
If you're going to stay.

I want you to know
That I truly love you
So please believe me
As I can't bare to be without you

I'll always be yours
And I wish you'd stayed mine
Baby don't worry
Everything'll be fine

Everything'll work out
Just wait and see
I don't have any doubts
So please believe me

I love you truly
I really do
So please believe me
When I say I want *you!*

Jane Hay

Secret Love

A tender look - a secret smile
I hold my breath, and for a while
I belong to you

A warm caress - a gentle kiss
I close my eyes and make my wish
- To belong to you

A caring hug - I hold on tight
Knowing this can't last all night
I have to go

I long to stay and feel you near
I wipe away a secret tear
I hate to go

I sit alone with thoughts of you
That stir up feelings deep and true
- I long to belong to you

Sue Freeman

Untitled

You came into my life
Bringing happiness and light
From the moment I met you
I knew that you were right

Each day that passes
I love you more and more
Where once there were just walls
There's now an open door

I look forward to our future
And the life that we will share
With the comfort of knowing
That you always will be there

And I'll be here for you
Every hour of every day
Forever by your side
Is where I plan to stay

So here's to us my love
And the path we walk together
Each tiny step we take
Is a step towards forever

Sara Bailey

Ghost Lover

I can hear his footsteps behind me,
But I know there's nobody there.
I feel his warm breath on my shoulder,
And the pain is too much to bear.

I yearn for his presence around me,
And the caresses that I once knew.
His warm gentle arms that once held me,
His kiss so tender and true.

I sense his body brush by me,
My feelings I cannot conceal.
I reach out, for him to hold me,
With a passion that's almost unreal.

I can hear his laugher surround me,
But soon it has faded away.
But the words that he whispered, stay with me,
We'll be together - my love, one day.

Diane Burgess

Only You

Only for you will my sun shine
Over those grey cloudy days

Only for you will my laughter ring
To chase away those troubles

Only for you will my desire burn
To satisfy your hunger

Only for you will my body yearn
Because for me there is no other

Only you.

Denise Emeny

Untitled

I wake up in the morning,
And right away feel blue.
Because something deep inside me
Says today I won't see you.

Still I plod along,
Doing things I have to do
Each chore seems even harder
Because I don't have you.

Oh how much time is left
Each hour seems like two
I'll never go away again
Unless I go with you.

Kathleen Southall

Rejection

I was cast aside
Like an autumn leaf
Blowing so listless
Hiding my grief

Strong blizzards came
Frost - covered snow
Cold as my heart
No feelings to show

Snow drops appeared
A crocus peeped through
The sun shed promise
Of a soft spring dew

Then April showers
Softened my heart
My pain was easing
Since we had to part

Now with summer's radiance
I dance on sweet grass
Your memory lingers
All bitter things pass

Georgina Oregan

With Love X

W hy did I have to fall in love? It turned my life around,
my head was floating in the clouds, my feet were off the ground.
I could not eat, or sleep, or think, my mind was in a whirl,
you smiled at me, you touched my hand, you said I was your girl.
T he days were bright and happy, magic times when we would meet,
treasured moments belonged to us, our love made them complete.
H appiness was ours my love, as our passion reached the sky,
I never thought the day would come, when you would say good-bye.

L ove and trust I gave to you when we became as one,
your every whim I tried to please, my life just flowed along.
O utcast, when you found new love, and I was last to know,
then my poor heart broke in two, when you told me I must go.
V ery slowly I have learned to function just as one,
my lonely days seem endless, my nights so dark, and long.
E veryone was very kind, they said the hurt would heal,
but they can't feel what my heart feels, this feeling so unreal.

X eno, is the life I have, delight, your constant mood,
I'll never understand this strange emotion known as love.

Hazel Collins

To Paint in Words

(To Sheila)

I regret that words must fail
in my expression of love for you
and yet from the depths
of my poetic soul
I have ploughed and harrowed
syllabic soil
until sweat broke upon my brow
forcing me to lay aside my tool
and try again another day
to paint in words my love for you.

Liam O'Comain

The Meaning of Love

The word love means so many different things,
Such as love of cream cakes, the love of rings,
I'd love to have this, I'd love to have that,
I love your new shoes, I love your new hat.

But sincere and deep love is none of these,
It's caring for someone, trying to please,
Meeting your true love, your heart skips a beat,
Now at long last to be swept of your feet.

Marriage vows taken, promise to be true,
Said from the heart just from me, just for you,
Love of your children, they are your whole life,
They stem from the love shared as man and wife.

As the years rush by, and youth fades away,
True love still deepens with each passing day,
Wisdom in knowing what love really means,
Loving memories recalled, beautiful scenes.

But the love which is true, constant by far,
In my darkest moments, my brightest star,
The greatest of love there ever could be,
Is my love for God and his love for me.

S M Stock

Love

I love my mum,
And I love my dad,
My brother too,
Who isn't that bad!

I love my gran,
And grandad too,
I love our birds,
(One's green, one's blue).

I also love,
Our cockatiel,
And I'd love a hamster,
With a light blue wheel.

Rachel L Watkins (11)

Come Now With Me Love

See how the moonlight
Caresses the water,
Traces a pathway,
A silvery stream.

Hear how the pulse of
The ocean is gentle,
Murmuring softly,
And ready to dream.

Breathe in the perfume
Of deep-scented roses,
Drifting around us
Like mist never seen.

Feel how our hearts beat
In tune with each other,
Lips touching, blending
Sweetly forever.

Come now with me, love,
Along the bright moonbeam,
Hands clasped together,
Our futures entwined.

Margaret Giacomini

Chemistry

I understand it's chemistry
destroying my serenity
I understand it wasn't planned -
it simply had to be
But please explain - just once again
why you, why us, why me?

I feel that it's your gentleness,
or is it just your sweet caress -
your honest eyes, your lullabies?
I simply cannot guess.

It puzzles me that I am drawn
to you, for reasons still unknown
This game of love's a mystery
Yet still it keeps enticing me.

I'm curious to know, it's true,
why me, why us, why you?

Lyn Aspinall

Love Unconditional

So deep is my bond with you
Your ailments make me suffer too
Your bare skin bereft of fur
Makes me shudder, eyes a blur
Biting scratching in one place
Leave me feeling desolate

So when I think you are in pain
I call the good vet yet again
You hate him now with all your might
But without him a sorry sight
You would look for all the ills
With which your tiny frame's been filled

And yet your beauty never wanes
Your silky tiger's pelt remains
Your amber gaze upon me rests
And purring comes from a white chest
I love to gently stroke and stroke
Even while I'm going broke
From paying for your necessities
Which I deem a privilege

Friends all know my greatest pleasure -
Devotion to my feline treasure

Rachel Silbert

Love on the Run

Kissing and cuddling
Love on the love,
Lips sometimes missing
Their passion to prove.
Doing a love twirl
In step with their feet
A boy and girl,
As lovers meet.
She with her fingers
In the back pocket, of his jeans;
Whilst his hand lingers
Where it shouldn't have been.
Side stepping obstacles in their embrace;
Love on the run a marathon race.

K Casewell

Love

Love makes you laugh, or makes you cry
Sometimes it just passes by.
When it touches, you'll soon know
As all those feelings stir below.

Your fingers tingle with a kiss
Your heart now a beat will miss.
Cupid's arrow hits the spot
As your stomach becomes a knot.

Holding hands, smoothing hair
All the signs of love are there.
But will it last, or will it fade?
Or was it in Heaven made?

Kathy Penberthy

The Bridge

Love builds bridges
Don't you know
And even though
You've got to go
My love has built a bridge
From my heart
Through to yours.
Love keeps things
Just alright
So even though
You are out of sight
My love burns
Deep within my heart
And keeps us close
While we are apart.

Dorothy Hayes

Each Day Brings More Sunshine

Lady with gentle, honest eyes
And radiant expression
Can you ever realise
How I treasure the deep impression
That loving you has carved inside
My very heart and soul
Please understand I've really tried
These emotions to control
I triumph for a little while -
On mundane matters dwell
But soon your captivating smile
Will work its magic spell
Again all thoughts are brought to bear
More intense than ever it seems
Upon a special lady fair
The subject of my dreams.

Gary Smith

Anguished Parting

Soft romantic music floats around this room
This dimly lit room where we have loved to dine,
A candle flickers on the corner table
Where first you told me that you were mine.

This night is the last we shall spend together,
I know that tomorrow we have to part,
These last precious hours I'll remember for ever
And cherish the memory deep in my heart.

As we now cling and dance to our favourite song
I feel your kiss on my brow and hear your sighs,
And I know I'll be haunted my whole life long
By the look of love that I see in your eyes.

Hold back the dawn while I beg you to stay,
I can't bear to hear your last *Goodbye*
Or watch you as you walk away
For a little of me will surely die.

For when you've gone and have left me all alone
Through all the days, the months, the years,
I shall see you again and the love we have known
As through a kaleidoscope edged with tears.

Nancy Sheldon

My Husband

I've only know the beauty
Of making love with you
I've only shared the passion
That comes with love that's true
I've only felt the tender touch
The touch of you alone
And love the moments that we share
When we are on our own
And if we never loved again
And you were no more mine
My body's had enough of you
For memories all through time

Sally McNab

When I'm Holding You

When first we went together,
Some it didn't seem to please,
They said incompatible,
Others chalk and cheese.

But it never put you off,
All this doubtful questioning,
You even said the differences,
Made it all the much more interesting.

And when we're sitting close.
And holding like we do,
They will never understand,
Of how I feel of you.

Like the sand upon the desert,
Like the salt in the sea,
Like the snow upon the mountain,
Like Sandra next to me.

Kevin Fitzgerald

Affair of the Soul

A moment we shared,
  A thought that cared,
A memory to last,
  Now the moment has passed.

A word and a smile,
  we were close for a while,
With no need to hold;
  In our affair of the soul.

A lot we have missed,
  Never hugged, never kissed,
We belong to others,
  could never be lovers.

But we'll meet again,
  on a far distant plane,
Then the moment of rapture,
  Will be ours, to recapture.

Brian Theobald

The Sting of Love

As I lay on the floor all soaking wet
I opened my eyes and there we met
How could you have been such a daft mug
To throw all the water from a jug
I'm sorry that you thought me bold,
But lady, you were out stone cold
A victim of a wasp's cruel sting
I couldn't wait for them to bring
A glass of water, he said, smiling,
Oh fickle heart, man so beguiling,
I now joined in your happy laughter,
This time remembered ever after,
With Cupid's arrow straight and true
I knew my love was just for you.

Marie Wood

A Few Simple Words . . .

You'll never know how I love you,
For words cannot express
The way I feel when you kiss me
Or enfold me in your caress,
You'll never know how my heart soars
When you tell me you'll never leave,
You'll never know how good it feels
To have someone in whom to believe.
A thousand words would not be enough;
Even if they were all true,
For nothing on earth could describe what it's like
To be loved, as I am, by you.

Robert Houghton

Three Little Words

Three little words, was all she said,
Three little words, which echoed in my head,
Three little words, more priceless than gold,
Three little words, with which my heart, was sold.

x xxxx xxx
I love you.

Chris Hennessey

The Gift of Love

When God gave out the gift of love
He gave a lot to you
When he gave out understanding
He knew who to give it to
He handed out some patience
And wrapped it all with care
And while he did this special thing
He had you standing there

(For my Husband Chris
With Love Tina xxxx)

Tina Hennessey

Thank You Babe

Thank you for being my friend babe, at a time when I needed you most,
for bringing me back to the present from living my life with a ghost,
thank you for listening to me babe, at a time when I needed to speak,
and thank you for being my strength babe, at a time I was feeling so weak,
thank you for bringing back sunshine, in a world that held only rain,
thank you for being you babe, and for making me whole once again,
thank you for making me laugh babe, at a time when life made me cry,
thank you for being my hope babe, there were times that I wanted to die,
so if you're ever alone babe, or if you ever feel blue,
just call out my name I'll be there babe, like you were when I needed you.

Lorraine Buck

You

In the teddy bear arms
  of childish dreams,
In the dark of warm sheets
  and soft blankets,
In the loose fitting folds
  of wrinkled love,

All I have of You.

Margaret Williams

Jealousy

Blood from the body,
Blood from the heart,
How can you stop something,
That you didn't start?

Sweat from the body,
Sweat from the head,
Sweat to mix with,
The blood that you've bled.

Tears from the body,
Tears from the heart,
Running now and forever,
From your bleeding heart.

Mac Reynolds

Love

My thoughts often stray,
As I ponder the day away,
Thinking of your touch,
I need you so very much.
My heart yearns for you every waking minute,
I cannot imagine my life without you in it.
Now we have found each other,
I do not want any other lover,
Let us always be together,
Loving each other forever and ever.

Diane Moore

Respect

Why don't you listen to me
Why don't you hear what I say
Is it because I'm invisible
That no attention you pay.

Why can't you see that I need you
Can't you see I love you lots
Please, please tell me that you care
Before our marriage rots.

I wish that you could understand
Just what I'm trying to say
Because I need you to respect my feelings
Before our love slips away.

Veronica Leedham

Still

Still am I breathless,
 Sensing you are near.
Still do I tremble
 Whenever you're here.
Still am I longing
 For none but your touch,
Still nought else moves me,
 I need you so much.

Still will I shadow
 Your every pace.
Still am I searching
 For want in your face.
Still will I never
 Relinquish hope till
Still is my heart beat.
 Still. Ever still.

Cherry L Tompsett

Valentine's Bridge

Two lovers leave
In light of morning sun;
No word nor sound
Is made between them,
Tender touch is all they share.

Cross meadows and o'er streams,
They hold each
On lonely walk
To the cause they must meet,
Upon the bridge of Valentine's.

Where on the foot they stand,
And far below a torrent.
When in the evening glow of sun
They leave their love in rapture;
Ghosts lost forever.

And off the bridge they step
And in the air they kiss
And in each heart they live;
Always two lovers,
On Valentine's bridge.

Robb Ives

The Angel and the Demon

You call me your precious, your love, your light,
Your beautiful woman who will guide you aright,
Let all the world hear my answer,
I am not afraid to say what I know to be true,
We are bound two souls together, I live and love but for you.

If you consider me an angel,
It is because we are bound also by God's heavenly laws,
And if you consider me an angel, then you also are the cause,
Willingly, I lay down my love at your feet,
Some woman does this every day, for a man she may meet.

Had you broken my heart or been untrue, this love that burns intensely for you,
Might have engulfed me in shame, made me less tender and fair,
Making you understand without even having to be told,
That angels and devils come from the same mould.

Man and the world can make grave mistakes in judging these things,
Great good and evil are born in us all, love guides us, or passes us by,
Provides us with wings, that will fail or fly.

But dear man you must take credit, for your loving influence,
You must thank your own worth, for what I have grown to be,
For the demon lurked very closely, to the angel in me.

Shirley Boyson

Untitled

My heart is pounding, beating fast,
Is ours a love that's meant to last?
Is this a love that's here to stay?
Can it last through rainy days?
For days I asked myself all this
And then I felt your loving kiss
The answers then were in my heart
We're never meant to be apart
I know that you can feel it too
For both our hearts run straight and true
Now we'll be together
Forever and a day
For only love that lasts a lifetime
Ever feels this way.

S Thompson

Dedicated to Beverley Price

You guided me as a parent,
On your strength I did depend,
And now as I'm growing up,
I'm glad you're my best friend!

You've helped with many choices,
My respect for you endures,
But we must learn to make decisions,
As our life matures!

Independence is a thing,
Which everyone must learn,
Through new responsibilities,
Our freedom we must earn!

Ironing, washing and cleaning our mess,
You're a miracle sent from above,
You make our home a happy place,
It's you we truly love!

Nicola Price

Love is it?

I looked for love and what did I find?
A situation where heart ruled mind.
A proposal accepted, the vows said *For Life*.
It was wonderful being somebody's wife

Family growing. A small happy crowd.
As time hopped along they made me feel proud.
I do love you I said to my spouse.
Alarm. More respond from the side of the house.

I walked in a circle. I felt like a clown.
Or a puzzled dog seeking a place to sit down.
Just what to do, knowing not where to start.
An appalling decision, we would have to part.

Remembering that day, it was suddenly so cold.
The dream crashed down. My image looked old.
The bed large and lonely, not at all warm.
Love. You could keep it. Brought nothing but harm.

Years later I looked at the world in its state.
It was up to the people. They must see they can't wait.
A solution for all must quickly be found.
Hope there's enough love for all to go round?

Violette Edwards

To B J

I was born when I met you
I have lived because you are with me
I will die when you leave me
So stay with me forever.

Terry Sherwin

Never Mind the Rain

It was cold that day
And so we left the train
Instead we took a taxi
So that we kept out of the rain

We got out of the taxi
And walked up the street
Our arms were around each other
And others thought it was sweet

Romance was in the air
And in the warmth of her arms
I felt a sense of pride
For I was captivated by her charms.

I'd leave to go home
But my heart would always stay
With the girl I wanted to be with
Each and every day

But like all good things it ended
And inside I felt the pain
Of a heart that broke in two
After walking in the rain

Barry Hobin

Love

When I first saw you it was love at first sight
I tried, I fought it with all my might
I lost, it's like asking the sun not to shine
I love you my darling will you be mine?

We have been together for over a year
To fathom out, I have not been easy I fear
When I have a problem you are always near
I love you so much, you will always be dear.

All is now said and done
You will always be my number one
This love of ours is everlasting
I will marry you, I will wear your ring.

Vanessa White

You

You'll always be on my mind,
In memory of the time we spent together,
The fun we had,
The love we shared,
You showed you cared,
And that you loved me,
You showed me I was special,
You taught me to be myself,
To show myself,
To trust others,
And to love you.

Wendy Poulter

Bandit Man

I set down these words with your pen
Borrowed, so that later when,
You read these poor lines
You may smile,
And know I was thinking of you
If just for a while.
Late at night, eleven thirty pm
I miss you already and the night seems long,
I miss you already and you're only just gone.

S Cowey

Straight From the Heart

When I look in your eyes, I feel on cloud nine,
I never would've believed,
That you would be mine.

My heart stops and misses a beat,
When your name is mentioned,
I feel weak from my head to my feet.

Your hands touch my soul,
Not just my body,
With you I have no control.

The winds stop above my head,
But the whole world moves,
For us, together, alone in bed.

Because of having you, each day is brighter,
I see gold in everyone and everything,
With you my fears become lighter.

Just as you are, from the heart - I love you,
And for being you,
I truly thank you.

Nikki Melton

Please Come Back

You said that you would always stay.
Now I am left without you.
Why did you have to go away?
I always think about you.

I pass your house, it looks the same,
Though now you are not there.
Is it me that is to blame,
And did you really care?

I thought you loved another,
Maybe it wasn't true,
But I shall always wonder
Whether I wronged you.

I need your arms around me,
To hear your tender voice,
Telling me you love me,
That I'm your only choice.

That day could be tomorrow,
Maybe it will never come.
But I shall always love you
Until my days are done.

Margaret Perrow

First Love

I first set my eyes upon you when I was still at school
You didn't even notice me, you acted very cool.
You asked to date a friend of mine, I really was up tight.
But I showed no jealousy, I cried most of the night
Lots of girls fancied you, you really turned them on.
You never took them seriously, you didn't keep them long
Then one day you asked me out, I was taken by surprise
That first kiss was everything, I thought I nearly died
We became the best of friends, no money could ever buy
Then one day you were gone, without even a sigh.
I've never got over it, I think of you all the time
I pray one day you will return, and that you may be mine
That was so long ago, but I do still remember
The sun was shinning brightly second of September
They say that the first love, is always the one, the best
Memories from it stands right out different from the rest.

Jan Nice

Loneliness

Why did you have to leave me?
And go so far away,
My life is empty without you,
Please come back and stay.

Remember the day I met you?
The sun was shining bright,
Remember the first kiss you gave me?
Under the July moonlight.

But all good things come to an end,
As the holiday soon passed by,
Standing at the harbour, with you in my arms,
We said our last goodbye.

I've been so sad and lonely,
Since the night you went away,
So please, my summer romance,
Come back to me and stay.

Debbie McMurray

Sweetness

Dear Sweet Husband you're so precious for sure,
And with your ways I love your more and more,
Like when your bring me tea at the crack of dawn,
It starts me off to a wonderful morn,
The way you help me throughout the day,
In your very own special way,
The way you say are you alright,
As I tip toe out of bed at night,
The way you fret when I'm not well,
Without you darling life would be hell,
So I thank you with all my heart,
And pray to God we'll never part.

L P Smith-Warren

A Brand New Start

My darling I do love you so
more than you will ever know.
You bring me sunshine all the time
no more pain is ever mine.
You lift me up when I am low
oh, I love you so.
You treat me like a rose petal
you make me feel so very special.
Please believe me when I say
Please don't ever go away.
You light a candle in my heart
For us it's a brand new start.
Oh my darling please do stay,
For I love you more than words can say.
If ever we should part
Just remember this brand new start.
So love me for ever more
Just like the petal on the shore.

Margaret Ellis

You

When you're around
  my feet don't touch the ground,
My heart aches and its beat does pound.
  This love of ours I'm glad we found,
Together we are strong,
  Our hearts beat as one.

If you should ever leave me,
  and your caress I could not keep,
The pounding from my heart
  Would surely miss a beat.
Then all that I could find
  to do would be to sit
and weep and weep.

Julie Anne Crew

Completing the Jigsaw

The missing link in my chain
Clasp me tight to your heart
Let me start to live again

The last drop in my ocean
Protect me from life's waves
Save me in my confusion

The strawberry for my cream
A fruit for all seasons
Squeeze me tight - prove you're no dream

The final piece of jigsaw
Completing the puzzle
Keep me whole, for ever more

Angela Gray

Valentine's Day

I used to spend my life feeling lonely and sad,
Thinking of all the love that I'd never had.
It seemed others had it all, yet I had none,
When was I going to start having some fun?

So many times I'd been hurt and just used,
No wonder I ended up feeling so confused.
But now all that is in the past,
Because I've found a true love that will last.
Special, loving and kind are all words to describe my man,
He's a guy who loves and accepts everything I am.

Now I've got someone to pick me up when I'm down,
And when I'm sad he will always be my clown.
When I need him, by my side he will stay,
And for the first time I won't be alone on Valentine's Day.

(Dedicated to Darren)

Andrea Fyfe

Straight From the Heart

Among your thoughts, tell me this
What do you call a kiss?
It is a delight of love
Between the lips so soft
Fed by warm desire or lust
It is an enchantment
Tempting all the passers by
Goddess of pleasure, youth and peace
Come in all shapes to love
And sigh and kiss as lovers do
Make the way smooth for me
And I could wish you all who love
That from your thoughts be free.

Dora Doyle

For the One I Love

To you I'd give the sky and sea
The birds that sing on every tree,
To you I'd give the fields of green
With all the flowers ever seen.
To you I'd give the rocks of grey
To safely guide you on your way,
To you I'd give the gentle brook,
And with it the mountain path it took.
To you I'd give the moon and sun
And with it the whole world as one.
But to you I give my very heart,
As mine, I have this to impart.
To you I give a love that's true,
It's meant my darling just for you.

Joan S Womersley

Love Under Will

Build a Fortress around your Heart
With gates of love so hard to part.

Let soldiers of volition guard within.
Love under will keep your soul from sin.

Paul Corrigan

Straight From the Heart

(Dedicated to Ashley Stratford)

I doubt I'd give the world to you,
for it's not mine to give.
And if I gave you everything,
I'd have no will to live.

Instead I thought I'd send to you,
Through the hill and dale.
A little something for you to treasure,
Each time you get my mail.

Always keep it close to you,
where ever you may be.
Because although it's not the whole world,
It's very dear to me.

Every time I write to you,
You'll receive another part.
Because it's just a little love,
But it's straight from the heart.

Lorna Livingston

Letters Directly From my Heart

Letters directly from my heart,
is my way of communication whilst we're apart.
I long for those happy days to return,
the very thought of you makes my crazy heart - churn.
Those first days of infatuation are impossible to forget,
thinking loving thoughts of my true love I hardly slept.
A voice inside yelled you are the one,
it seemed as if my life had just begun.
Your sweet smile, your romantic glance,
your affectionate touch made me want to dance.
Your presence near me was a delicious delight,
as the exploding fireworks within me were starting to ignite.
Writing all my emotions has made me remember,
all is not lost, we are meant to be together.
So don't make me any more blue, come back
to me my love for I will always love you.

Shafila Akhter

I Miss You

I can still remember
The day you walked away
My head told you to go
My heart longed for you to stay

Now I am left with a hole in my heart
That only you can fill
I just have to tell you
I know I love you still

It's been six years it seems like more
Oh why did you have to go
If you read my eyes, my lips, my heart
You'll know I love you so

I know I made a big mistake
I know we shared the pain
So please if you are reading this
I want you back again

Debbie Dabson

Keep Me in Your Heart

I left my girl for prison
And that I can't deny
I spent my time in solitary
And never blinked an eye
But no one knows my sorrows
Or the love I have inside
I shed my tears in silence
When others are asleep
But soon we'll be together
Never again to part
So 'til that day dear Sue
Keep me in your heart

Susan Kendrick

Tomorrow

This is a one off situation,
A moment to be lived and then passed.
This is the alpha and the omega,
This is the first and the last.
There's nothing special about you and I,
We're the proverbial ships in the night.
Tomorrow I know that this will be wrong,
But for now it is perfectly right.
Tomorrow I'll think *oh what a fool*
When I meet with the cold light of day
But for now I rejoice that you're here with me,
And I desperately want you to stay
But tomorrow I know you'll be drifting
After that road you're following down
So for now I'll sink slowly into the depths
Of your true blue eyes and drown.

Maureen George

Untitled

I awoke one morning and I realised you'd gone
I thought I had a dream and I heard our favourite song
I thought that you were with me and not so far away
I thought that you still loved me and you were back to stay
In my dream you loved me and you said you really cared
You loved me for the future and the memories we once shared
I saw you walking towards me and you looked with loving care
A kiss I felt you gave me as if you were really there
But now I know I had a dream and the sunlight turns to rain
For my heart is filled with sorrow and I just can't take the pain,
For dreams can be so special
So we'll make our dream come true
For I know we've got a special love
A love so rare, but true
So when I close my eyes tonight
And dream my dreams of you
I hope that in your heart tonight
You're dreaming of me too.

Geraldine McGuinn

First Love

I was only six and a bit, yet I shall never forget the day
I was Mary, and Richard was Joseph in our school Nativity Play.
Richard liked football, hated girls, but I loved him from the start
Told my best friend Amanda he would always be my sweetheart.

At fourteen, the prettiest girl in class was blonde Amanda Brown,
I cried buckets into my pillow after I saw her with Richard in town.
Out of all the boys in Standard IV, she could have had her pick,
Amanda was my best friend no more when I found she'd stolen Rick.

Three years later, in sixth form, came my long-awaited chance,
Richard asked me to be his date at the big school leaving dance.
I blushed as only a redhead can, and answered with little grace,
Why not Amanda? He grinned and said, 'I asked you, freckle face.'

I was up on Cloud Nine that evening, Rick only had eyes for me
But I knew three years was a testing time until he got his degree.
He said, 'You're my girl. I'll write.' I cried as we kissed good-bye
On the Campus there'd be many *Amandas* to tempt a good looking guy!

Almost fifteen years is a long time to wait, I trusted Rick and yet
Remember Romeo and Juliet, Adam and Eve, Scarlet O'Hara and Rhett?
But the best love stories end happily and in true story book style
Richard, my sweetheart was waiting when Dad walked me down the aisle.

Jo Elsome-Jones

Ode to a Cornish Maid

Her hair is the colour of a raven's wing
and her eyes are as dark as sloes,
in truth she is a Celtic Queen
who graces modern clothes
which she enhances with her form
so entrancing to the eye,
radiating voluptuous femininity
like a star in the velvet sky.

Lewis Rowe

If I Could Just Have You

I've built myself a dream world where I can be with you,
and if that dream world shattered my heart would break in two.

I dedicate every word to you, I dedicate this song,
read the words and you will see, baby I've waited so long.

My world is built around you, my feelings I can't hide,
come and find my world and come with me inside.

I'd never meet another, no, it just wouldn't be right,
I couldn't love some other, only you can hold me tight.

Come into my life, fall in love with me,
come into my heart, I'm handing you the key.

This world is open to you, come and discover it,
my heart is like a jigsaw, and you have the piece that fits.

My heart is filled with love for you, and I love you more each day,
if you ever broke my heart it would hurt me in every way.

I dream of me and you every single night,
please tell me what to do, I know it feels so right.

Come and discover a world of love, here in my heart,
don't go anywhere else or you'll tear this heart apart.

So listen to these words, every verse is true,
baby I wouldn't want anything, if I could just have you . . .

Claire J Young

Untitled

My dearest husband, sweetheart and best friend -
I love you in the night
I love you in the day,
I love you in the morning -
What else is there to say?

I love you in the springtime,
I love you in the fall,
But when we snuggle up -
Is the time I love best of all.

Betty Sims

Night Without Words

The only night I saw you,
We had no conversation.
We had champagne
And all the trimmings;
But we hardly spoke at all.

Five love-locked hours,
For me have lasted:
But for you, perhaps, forgotten
In a welter of boardroom meetings;
For we hardly spoke at all.

And if, by any happy chance,
I can engineer another meeting
And try to make you feel -
Would you? For we only felt each other,
And we hardly spoke at all.

Jenny M Humphrey

Lost Love

Echoes of another day,
the other life that slipped away,
and fell, lost for all time;
a cavern too deep to climb

Or scale away these bitter tears,
that shadow the fun that filled those years;
'til now I'm left alone and blue,
desperate to recall visions of you.

Simone Eade

Untitled

One thing remains to light my path
In those dark days of doubt and fear.
The knowledge of your love for me
That burns a beacon bright and clear.
A glow of glory in the doom
On which my eyes are ever set
Your faith in me - your constancy
These things I never shall forget.
This is the light by which I walked
When every other star had gone
This is the fire that warmed my heart
That lit my steps and spurred me on.

The knowledge of your deep devotion
And affection fond and true.
Much have I lost but this remains.
Your love for me
And mine for you.

Joyce Melrose

Appealing

Fan our love into flame -
Don't let us part -
There's more than an ember -
Here in my heart -

When we quarrelled I know -
I was to blame -
Forgive me and Darling -
Fan our love into flame -

All the while as I dream -
Of your wonderful charms -
I long to embrace you -
Close in my arms -

I am hoping that you -
Will feel the same -
Come back to me Darling -
Fan our love into flame.

S C Humphrey

A Mother's Love

You are always there
 on you I can depend.
All through my life
 my dearest friend.
Yours is a love
 that is oh so rare.
Showing each day
 you really do care.
Comforting and loving
 holding my hand.
Smiling and knowing
 you understand.
You gave a lifetime of love
 I will always treasure.
Mother your love
 is beyond any measure.

(For my mother, Alice Davies.
Thanks mum for being you)

Jacqueline Hall

Thank You for Caring

When someone takes the time to listen,
  When someone reaches out,
When someone does a thoughtful thing,
  That makes you warm throughout.

When someone lends a helping hand,
  Find ways in which to share,
When someone makes you feel secure,
  By always being there.

When someone senses there are times,
  When you have special needs,
When someone gives you inner strength,
  Through words as well as deed.

When someone seems to take an interest,
  In just how you're faring,
It's time to tell that special someone,
  Thanks so much for caring.

Helen Quish

Summer Loving

The waves ripple up to the sand
As we walk hand in hand,
From the distance we see the sunset
As our feet begin to get wet,
We walk slowly along the beach
There is no need to teach,
You know all there is to know
About the sun and water flow,
The breeze is cool
As you swim in the pool,
Of shining sea
Made for you and me.

Sarah Ellery

It's Funny How . . .

It's funny how that impish grin
Complete with seasoned eyes
Are all essential ingredients
For Heart's Desire pie.

It's funny how that throaty laugh
And bashful little smile
Give the dish that splash of *mm!*
Turning taste buds wild.

It's funny how those simple words
So plain and straight but true
When sprinkled in the mixing bowl
Cause new sensations untrue!

It's funny how this recipe
So full of *naughty but nice*
With definite Heavenly origins
Is a real live Earthly Delight!

S J Armah

The List

I see those eyes so crystal clear
And fall within your soul.
A raging torrent pulls me in,
It's hard to keep control.
Those lips are so inviting,
I linger there with ease.
No thoughts of any other,
You're the one I wish to please.
The lobes that dangle brightly,
My amusement for to catch.
You think it strange I watch them,
It's just one endearing patch.
The neck is sleek and slender,
Screaming for a kiss,
If we should e'er be parted
That section I would miss.
The rest is pure delightful,
A pleasure to the brain
But the beauty there is secret
So from writing I refrain.

Carl Robinson

The Prettiest Rose

Its beauty came from within the earth,
Upon a tree that grew so green,
First it budded then it bloomed!
The prettiest rose you have ever seen,
I admired its fine splendour as I watched it
Grow and grow!
Then smelt its fragrance on the wind
When it began to blow!
It reminded me of passionate love,
That comes to youth in bloom,

It made me think of life itself
That starts within the womb!
It made me think how we're like flowers
That blossom then we die
And are blown away to be forgotten
As time goes by and by!
But that prettiest rose reminded me
Of my sweetheart who's oh so fair!
So I plucked it from that fine green tree
And placed it in her hair.

Michael David Sparkes

Adieu

I remember
Sun shining
Spirits high
You and I

I remember
Softly raining
Gentle grin
Let me in

I remember
Showers streaming
Jacket shared
Know you cared

I remember

Jan Jones

If . . .

If I never called again
and strict silence did maintain
would this seem to you unfair?
Would you care?

If I said no word was true
of my messages to you
and I meant to be unkind,
would you mind?

If I never wrote a line
and gave no more the sign
of the hours I wish to share,
would you despair?

If I cut my heart in two
and your half away I threw,
as if we'd never met,
would you forget?

If the truth of all is this,
you dare not in a kiss
admit that love may grow,
would I know?

George Pearson

Dungeons of our Minds

Together we built castles
With rooms for all our dreams
But somehow we both faltered
Our dreams weren't what they seemed.

In each castle, we hid skeletons
So our dreams began to fade
If only we'd built trust instead
Then our future we'd have made.

Around our secrets we built barriers
As each room we both explored.
For our deceptions we chose silence
Respect for feelings we ignored.

But without commitment we were nothing
So we walked the dungeons of our minds
There's no longer rooms of happiness
Only ruins, we can find.

D Masterson

Loving Eyes

Just look at me with eyes that warm to words of simple praise
So heaven I can visualise through the mystery in your gaze.
Just look at me and let me see
That when you smile you smile of me
And in that look so warm and knowing
The love that glows - for me is glowing.
That I may penetrate the look
That reached out once and my heart took.

Such beauty in the wine red lips I ever yearn to kiss
And lose myself in swirling breathless, Niagara eddying bliss.
Just let me sink sublime, serene
In flight o'er mount'nous valleys green
And drown within that rapturous dwelling
Where words are known but need no telling.
O sweet warm precious, omniscient eyes
I seek no other paradise . . .
Beyond the rubicund of desire and joy
This Phoenix loves you with the wonderment of a boy.

Malcolm Burrows

I Love You

Love is a treasure
Enriched in gold
Forever wanting to hold
A ray of sunshine
Always a happy smile
Those are the things
That make you stand out a mile.

Pulse rating at your touch
Heart beating ever so much
Your gentle voice
Sending shivers through my spine.
Your guiding hand, and caring ways
Those are the things that make
you special in every way.

Because of your thoughtfulness all through
I love you you know that I do.
It would really mean the world to me
To have for life someone like you.
So please! Please be mine
And make my dreams come true
'Cause I love you - honestly I do.

Dympna Murray

The Enigma of Love

What was it that made us meet that night,
That took my life to a new heavenly height?
And what was it that made you glance,
That captured my heart, that's now set in a trance?

Who decided that in each other we should confide,
To open our hearts and no secrets to hide?
And who decided what action was to be done,
To ensure that both of us now became one?

How can it be that I turn hot then cold,
That when I hold you my emotions unfold?
And how can it be when snuggled up at night,
That when there is darkness, there is light?

Why is it just when we are on the right track,
A detour arrives and pushes us two steps back?
And why is it when I feel I want to walk out the door,
An alarm bell rings and I see your beauty once more?

Hywel Palmer

His Secret Smile

His secret smile tells me he knows,
As I walk down the aisle in lace
That with each day our sweet love grows.

I carry but one crimson rose,
Its blush reflects upon my face.
His secret smile tells me he knows.

He did not woo me with sweet prose,
Or words in sand his fingers trace
That with each day our sweet love grows.

Enough to know *'twas me he chose,*
Fine words for him are out of place.
His secret smile tells me he knows.

I understand deep his love flows
When, in his wordless warm embrace,
That with each day our sweet love grows.

As single hood draws to its close,
His hand in mine, my pulses race.
His secret smile tells me he knows
That with each day our sweet love grows.

C Morgan

Plighted

Not for me the shining armour
Or the arrowed Cupid's bow
I would rather that the showman
Keeps the light down low . . .
Not for me the words of amour
Glib and hearty they can be
I would rather that the love glow
Can be felt surrounding me . . .
All my life I have been waiting
Just for you, with thoughts endeared
By your ever warming presence
Nothing ventured, nothing feared . . .
You will always be my sweetheart
With a charm all of your own
Never leave me my beloved
For my love has grown and grown . . .

Margarette L Damsell

The Seasons of Love

Love in June is
summer's gold,

Love in autumn's
hard to hold;

Love in winter's
for the old,

But, love in spring is
. . . everything!

Janet Brown

Lawrence

The first time I saw him
a show off - oh so smart
little did I know then
he would steal my heart

We'd loads of fun together
unhappy times as well
did we marry far too young?
only time would tell

Then in time a family
Oh how years do fly
with two daughters we were blessed
the apple of his eye

I love him more as time goes by
my love will never end
so thoughtful wise and kind is he
my husband - and best friend

Joyce Battey

A Glenariff Love Poem

A ribbon of smoke on the fragrant breeze,
Drifts up the valley o'er the maze of trees,
And down by the fire a couple lie,
Wrapped in each other as the world stirs by.

The August sun has retired to bed,
And left a twilight of orange and red,
And down in the glade their young faces glow,
As the flames of their love begin to grow.

Rising in union their fusion is made,
The blaze has been quenched and the colours fade,
And spangled with stars the blanket of night,
Covers their slumbers 'til morning brings light.

Paul Hutton

Love is

We can fall in love
And out of love.
Love can be madness
Also such sadness.
Some like to flirt
Other's get so hurt.
Love is like honey
Some love for money.
We dream of love
Often die for love.
We yearn for it.
We fight for it.
Love is to care
Which can be rare.

Nancy Eleanor Smith

Love in Simple Terms

Love to me is everything from rosebuds blossoms grow,
Love is like the glistening in the crispy snow,
It warms your heart with a healthy glow,
It will always highlight my life no matter where I go,

The love you show your child is so inexpressible to me,
But a mother's love just fills your heart full of glee,
The love you show your partner is simply wonderful to find,
It relieves all the pressures of the daily grind,
Love is truly wonderful always let it be said,
A lover's open arms welcoming the day you wed.

It should last through all eternity grow richer year by year,
In between the sad times love wins through every tear,
Brings joy to every heart throughout the land,
Oh! the simple word love, it is so truly grand . . .

Denise Frost

Loneliness of Love

The days are long and lonely,
Ever since you've gone,
The nights are worse than ever
As the radio plays our song.

Why did it have to happen,
Why did you say goodbye,
Every time I think of you
I just begin to cry.

Love, it was the greatest gift
That we both did share,
You were my first and only love,
And now you are not there.

People try to comfort me
Saying *Plenty more fish in the sea*
But why can't they realise,
You were the only one for me.

Today I saw you both together,
Smiling, as you walked hand in hand,
I used to be her best friend,
And now to her, you have returned.

Catherine McVeigh

Flame Lit Reflections

Misery by candlelight,
Affected glances with disdain,
Tender touches turned frostbite,
Loving arms filled with pain.

When the candle wax has melted
Does it really symbolise the end?
Has the furnace of our love been smelted
With burning hearts no more to mend?

When draws the bloody battle to a close?
Who sounds the horn for our retreat?
Bearing cuts that do not show,
Never daring to admit defeat.

Maybe once I might have known
Which would be the wisest plan.
But my insecurity has grown
Along with follies of this man.

So I raise my head and smile,
Hoping that the strain's not seen.
I snuff the candlelight awhile,
And pretend that this has never been.

Rachel Louise Dunne

Summer Love

My heart began to miss a beat,
As I saw you in the summer heat,
Then I felt you touch my skin,
Your warm caress made me tremble within;
With eyes so bright but yet so deep,
The memory is mine to keep,
Our bodies are intertwined,
We join in heart, in soul, in mind,
In my dreams your face I see,
Through the night,
Sharing your love with me,
The days were slipping slowly by
And though our love will never die
The sunshine soon drew to an end
Farewell to you my love, my friend.

Pamela Stirling

Sweet Dream

I dream of a lover,
A lover so fine.
But how does she look,
This lover of mine.

Well her face is an oval,
Her breasts are upturned,
Her legs they are slender,
Her rear it is firm.

Her hair it is soft,
Her eyes a pale blue,
Her skin is like velvet,
Her love it is true.

Her voice it is gentle,
Her teeth they are fine,
Once a dream - Now she's real,
And this diamond, is mine!

Steve Bergin

Valentine's Day

V is for Valentine and Venus goddess of love
A is for adorable my husband whom I love
L is for love, which he gives to me
E is for Eros the anagram of rose
N is for the notice he always takes of me
T is for thought and troubles we share
I is for initials of which be both now share
N is for the nice things and knowing we both care
E is for eternity and everlasting love
S is for the sweet things and seasons that we share

D is for darling and knowing that I care
A is for always knowing I'll be there
Y is for yours forever and ever, and also
   The years we'll spend together

G J Danter

The Last Evening

In the hush of a late September evening, we watched
The tide turn - at the closing of the day.
A huge moon spread a golden path, across the heaving waves:
And seemed to know, we found *Goodbye* impossible to say.

A small cloud brushed across her brilliance: as if
In sympathy - to cast a shadow on our misery.
I took your hand in mine, as we stood in silence
- Just listening to the sighing of the sea.

Over now, our stolen days together - for we were not free:
And knew that, very soon, we had to part.
I wondered, was it spray - or tears - that glistened on your cheek?
As the breaking waves, disguised the pounding of my heart.

Gaenor Spratley

Ah Lisa

It's your eyes that get to me,
they shine like pebbles,
in a sea of constant beauty.
Your hair that flows down your back,
like waves breaking against the shore
and your smile and laugh,
put me under your spell just like witchcraft.
Ah but Lisa, it's those eyes that get to me.
Fight as I must my thoughts still scream for lust,
but like sand on a sand dune,
my thoughts blow away into nothing but dust,
but Lisa, your eyes still get to me.

P F Masterson

Happy Days

We crammed a lifetime of loving
Into the three short years we had.
We knew from the start we'd have to part,
But agreed to be happy, not sad.

We walked barefoot in morning dew,
Made love on sun-baked sands.
Stayed all day in bed when we wanted to;
Went everywhere holding hands.

We laughed and cried together;
Sometimes we talked all night.
We'd tell each other all our fears,
And wake up in the morning light.

Now you've gone to a better life,
I must make a brand new start.
When you were here I could be brave,
Now there's a rainbow in my heart.

I keep your love inside my soul,
Your child grows in my womb,
The love we shared was not in vain,
Happy days will be back soon.

Carole Brookes

Wonderful Dream

I press my head
lovingly where
in green spring grass
you spread your hair
and dream
you whisper in my ear
such tender words
so sweet and clear
it seems you still
are here.

I lift my head
and you are there
in green spring grass,
sun-haloed hair
caressing my face,
your lips meet mine
as together we kneel,
our kisses divine -
and my wonderful dream
is real!

Pat Cowlishaw

Eternal Equal

You occupy my thoughts
invade my dreams,
my mind is in constant turmoil
yearning silently to feel your tender touch
or hear your loving voice,
sweet words which flow endlessly
to send quivers down my spine
in eager anticipation,
the sound of your name alone
fills me with desire,
I long for your presence
so we both may be one
transfixed in each other's arms forever.

B J Harrison

Destiny

I thought
Perhaps
It won't be the usual fling.

Magically, inexplicably
It blossomed into the genuine thing.

Previous heartbreak faded into the past
Here was something inspired to last

No secrets, no lies
Just look into my eyes
Misty with tenderness
Pupils dilated with desire

I know it
You know it

We're in *love* and on fire.

Doreen Duce

First Love

He was five years old and handsome,
for the others we would wait
but always ended up together
swinging on our garden gate.

Sharing secrets amongst sun dried grass
Giving magic with tangled wild flowers for me,
Then bashful, he'd run, showing off
to skim higher up the gnarled old tree.

Imagination made dandelions yellow moons
Juicy woodland strawberries our summer wine,
How small hands held, and captured moments
which would not dissolve with time.

Days so tender were the promise
just a whisper and it's gone,
Most treasured chapter in life's pattern
but then first love must move on.

G Price

My Heart

My heart is like a golden chain
Which links my heart together
If you should break this chain
You'll break my heart forever.

My heart belongs to you
Like yours belongs to me
You are someone very special
In my heart you'll always be.

My heart can only love one person
That someone happens to be you
I just hope your heart
Can only love me too.

My heart leaps around inside me
Because I love you so much
When we're apart
I long for your touch.

My heart is very breakable
So don't ever go away
All my heart wants
Is for you to always stay.

Amanda Parfitt

Love Unrequited

Before I knew love unrequited
Thoughts of true love made me excited
I'd meet him at noon and pretty soon
To his home I would then be invited.

The day I met this gorgeous fellow
Looking my best all in yellow
Feeling so smart it would sure melt his heart
As he kissed me it really was heaven.

He murmured my name, his eyes were aflame
It could only be love at first sight
The future looked rosy, we two were so cosy
At last, I had met *Mr Right.*

Our next date, he was late
This can sometimes happen
But, no kiss, what was this?
Things followed the same pattern.

I waited and waited, my love unabated
Of him I saw not a glimpse
My love had departed, I'm left brokenhearted
Will romance always finish like this?

Doreen Gardner

Love

Love is what matters,
Love is what counts,
When you have worries,
When you have doubts.

Face it alone,
Of course you'll feel low,
Face it together,
See how it will go.

Another beside you,
Will make you feel strong,
So get it together,
And face what is wrong.

Eve Chapman

The Hayfield

The time passed slowly long ago.
We lay beneath the sky
And watched the shadows chase the sun
As summer clouds passed by.
Moon-daisies powdered us with gold,
The mower clacked away;
We did not heed it; we were young,
With time enough to stay.

Time passes quickly now I'm old.
I lie upon my bed,
But daisies on your resting place
Their golden dust still shed.
The sweet hay scents the murmurous air,
The mower still clacks by,
But where we dreamed the hours away
Now other lovers lie.

Betty Morris

Love

How can love be defined?
How can love survive?
Love is giving, sharing,
This keeps love alive.

Mary E Beale

Heartbeat

We two are lovers our hearts are entwined,
I shall be yours always, you will be mine,
Together we'll journey thro' life's upwards hill,
Until we reach our transcending idyll,
You gaze upon me so ardent with love,
I look upon you, only you I think of,
Time spent together, these memorable hours,
Walking through woods, 'mid sunshine and showers.
Hearts beat in unison, rhythm as one,
Poetry in motion, lovemaking is fun,
Emotions cause senses to tingle and quiver,
Soft sweet caresses that thrill with a shiver.
With your tender embraces, kindness and charm,
I know you will always keep me from harm,
I surrender to you, my beating heart misses,
As I give myself up to your vibrant kisses.

Glenda Lawrence

Straight From the Heart

Darling, will you love me forever?
Forever and a day?
When the sun shines bright
And when the sky is grey?
Thinking of you drives me crazy;
Sunny days become quite lazy;
Life's path is entirely mazy
While we're apart, my lovely Daisy!
          You are my heart's desire!
          Such is the consuming fire
          Of my love for you,
          Say you'll marry me soon,
          Or from grief I will expire!
The red roses are for love,
The pansies are for thoughts,
The honeysuckle for affection,
But with orange blossom I'll escort
You down the aisle, along to our Home Port!

Claude A Knight

Love Letters

Loneliness knows it not
Orders cannot command it
Vanity estranges it
Egotism kills it.

Clive Cornwall

My Love

My Love, what are you to me?
        Like sun after rain,
        Or relief after pain.
        Calm following unrest,
        All that is best.
You're everything nice, you see.

        Harmony after discord,
        Interest when I'm bored,
        Rest after toil;
        Peace not turmoil.
Feelings that will never change, I'm sure.

        Happiness after tears;
        Courage banishing fears.
        Laughter not a frown
        You raise me up when down.
You are all this - and more!

Margaret W Parsons

Footprints in the Snow

I wonder do you think of me
Does my memory haunt your mind
Back to days so long ago
To days when love was blind.

December snow was falling
On the day I watched you go
But all you left behind that day
were footprints in the snow.

My lonely heart went with you
You didn't feel it there,
The street was cold and empty
With nothing left to share.

I held you fast before you left
Yours were the arms that let go,
Now thinking of you all I see
Are footprints in the snow.

The stars now seem so far away
The moonbeams pale and gone,
And snowdrops harbingers of spring
Keep memories lingering on.

Wesley Price

To a Valentine

Love is a many splendoured thing
Of this I am so sure
It numbs the brain and fires the heart
There isn't any cure.

But may I say just one thing
My heart will never mend
For you'll always be my Valentine
I'll love you to the end.

Barbara Finch

To be in Love

Alive and vibrant, radiant, content,
Each day's joy is without measure,
The words *I love you* are really meant,
For someone who gives you nothing but pleasure.

A permanent daze, unable to think,
Living in a state of constant bliss,
When with each other, you become one link,
In a chain of warmth, sealed by a kiss.

There are times when apart, gloomy days,
Desperate to hear and see and touch,
A message, a letter, a word of praise,
These small things can mean so much.

Reunited again, you hug and embrace,
Wanting to hold each other so tight,
In the game of life you both hold an ace,
Never was anything quite so right.

If love finds you, how lucky you'll be,
To be given this special gift in life,
To have and to hold 'til eternity,
When you become husband and wife.

C Needham

While You're Away

These words I write cannot express
the feelings in my heart.
It seems to ache a little more
each second we're apart.
I long to take you in my arms
and tell you of my love.
And feel your flesh so pure and white
like the feathers of a dove,
Then to kiss your soft red lips
a taste of fine red wine
A symbol of my love for you
forever and devine.
Like the band of gold
upon your second finger in,
You and I together
whatever life may bring

Alan Denne

Straight From the Heart

My heart is broken, I feel such pain,
Am I never to see you again
All those promises you made to me
Cannot, or never, will be
I thought my future was secure
Instead of which I must endure
This yearning deep inside
From which I cannot hide
You betrayed me with such charm
Now I'm filled with alarm
Friends will say, we told you so,
But I couldn't say no
I loved you so much
You only had to touch
And I was filled with rapture
For my heart, you did'st capture
Goodbye, goodbye, to my dreams
Ah! Life is not always what it seems.

Eleanor Friston

Why?

I think of nobody but you,
Every night and every day,
I'd love to sit and listen -
To hear what you have to say.
Even though I love you,
You have no feelings for me,
Your feelings are for someone else,
Our love will never be.
I have my hopes deep down inside,
That your feelings really were
False lies, and untruths,
And one day you'll forget her.
But when I see you together,
My hopes are torn apart.
When I see, your lips touch,
You break my love-filled heart.
My feelings are so strong,
I only wish you knew,
After all this painful time,
Can't you see I love you?

Gianna Pollero (15)

Visions of Love

I have a love to match the World, words could never explain,
Although I lived on this planet for a million years, it could never
happen again.
For the beauty in your eyes, would never be matched I know,
The faith that burns from your eyes, would set this World aglow.

For everytime you smile at me, my poor heart does miss a beat,
I see you when I awake, always appearing in my sleep,
Your smile is like a thousand hands, that reach right out to me,
And although I was bound by the strongest chains, your smile
would set me free.

Your voice is like a nightingales, when she starts to sing,
Your hair so smooth and silky, reminds me of a new born spring,
When I see you in the mornings, while fresh dew is on the bough,
Your beauty radiates once more, and a peace is within me now.

In these times when I am sad, feeling down and blue,
Those visions of you return to me, with a tenderness and love
so true,
And every time you leave me alone, my spirit dies too,
For in this World I'll never find, like the love I have for you.

Jim Wilson

Death of a Lover

Oh fly on the wings of a swallow
or fly on the wings of a dove
and depart not 'til the morrow
depart not 'til the morrow my love

Stay by me and hold me with passion
the warmth of your body be mine
I will soar on the wings of an eagle
to die with my hand holding thine.

Ron Grantham

Quest for Love

The biggest regret that I have in my life.
Is the time that it took me to meet my wife

All those years, we spent apart.
Waiting for an arrow to pierce our hearts.

We led separate lives, oblivious of each other
Looking for a partner . . . we'd never bother

There's so much to do, and very little time
To be tied down now, would be a crime

I had long hair, she had short skirt's
Her leg's drove me wild, that I thought I must flirt.

I hope she'll say yes, when I ask her to dance.
A friend said, 'Don't bother you haven't a chance.'

But I took no notice of my friend you see, and that's
why this chic is married to me.

She's been my partner for twenty odd years.
So hard luck mate! stop shedding those tears.

We've two of a family, my, how they've grown.
Soon they'll be gone, then it's back on our own.

Just the two of us again, me and my wife.
I can flirt with her again, for the rest of my life.

Colin Mills

Troubled Waters

Let me ride the waves of hope,
and for a while pretend to cope
with mundane tasks, and useless schemes,
aborted plans, and shattered dreams.

Let me hang on to that world
where life was love, and love unfurled
the happiness within my soul,
releasing feeling, making whole.

Let me drift on seas of calm,
forgetting actions which caused harm.
Remembering how life used to be
before she took the place of me.

Let me go, I need to live,
love again, be free to give
at least as much as once before
- perhaps I should have given more.

Wendy Morris

You Are

You are the strength in my purpose,
You are the beat in my heart,
You are the whole of my being,
I miss you when we are apart.

You are the air that I breathe,
You are the sun in my sky,
You are the smile on my face,
And the happiness tear in my eye.

You are the breeze in my morning,
You are my moon shining bright,
You are the one that I lean on,
With you I just know I'm alright,

You are my power and glory,
You are my foundation strong,
You are the one who is right,
Without you I know I'd go wrong,

You are the colourful blossom,
That grows in my garden of life,
I would be no good here without you,
Thank you my wonderful wife.

Darrell Ryan

My Heart

If I could say what is in my heart
Then you and I would never part
For there's none so blind as those that can't see
We were made for each other, you and me
When we're apart, I'm half alive
Try as I may, I can't survive
I know deep down you feel the same
For I dearly wan't you to take my name
But I let my fears get in the way
For I'm so afraid that you won't stay
So my darling here I am
For now I've asked you to take my hand.

V A Skelton

My Dream Man!

I've been searching for a long time
For a man who's young and free,
Who is big and strong and handsome
And will take good care of me.
I'm looking for a partner
Who is tender, kind and caring,
Who knows that life's made richer
By helping and by sharing.
I want a guy who's trendy,
Who likes the latest fashion.
I need someone who will love me
With a deep abiding passion.
I need a man who's gentle
As well as being strong,
I want someone who'll forgive me
If I do something wrong.
I want a man who really loves me
And who'll be forever true,
But the best blokes are all taken,
So I guess I'm stuck with you!

June Stokes

Impossible Love

A goddess, an angel standing there
Perfectly formed long flowing hair
The result of artistic duty
You stand alone in innocent beauty.

Venus herself would envy you
From the purest of marble you grew
Oh! ethereal creature of icy heart
My soul you entrapped from the start.

From your magnetism I cannot sway
My feelings for you, I cannot display
Placed before you in eternal trance
On winged feet frozen in dance.

My love for you can never be
Your unseeing eyes, will never see
As I reach for you with unfeeling hand
I too, on a pedestal eternally stand.

Sue Jackson

True Love

True love is gentle, kind and warm, tender pure and true,
It's something more precious than gold, priceless through and
through.
It's finding joy in what we give, being patient when one's low,
It tries to understand one's needs, showing love that's all aglow.
Being ready to give that helping hand, to brush away those tears.
To give that love that's true and kind, it takes one's fears.
True love is not a selfish love, it's making one's heart glad,
To see the joy it brings to one, thats heart is feeling sad.
True love is always ready, to forgive and forget,
Holds no malice in one's heart, no feelings of regret.
So if we are looking for such love, that's pure, kind and true,
Let's be sure that we can give, that love to others too.

V Eastwood

Opposites Attract

I admire your dark brown hair
Even though myself I'm fair
I love your deep hazel eyes
Though mine are blue like the sky

You are tall, I'm petite
You are strong, I'm small and sweet

You are tanned
I am very pale
You're so muscular
I'm so frail

My hair is short, yours it's long
I am soft, you are strong.

They say opposites attract
I'm attracted to you that is a fact
It doesn't matter if in common we've nothing
'Cause I'm sure gonna give you all my loving.

Mandy Jane Ackerman

On Your Shore

From within me calls:
Could it be I'm dreaming?
So in love with you,
The sensation leaves me reeling.
On your shore I'm walking,
With you close beside me,
A hand gives a hand,
Trusting fingers entwine,
On your shore I'm smiling,
As the bad times fall behind.

Patrick Hennessy

Our Love of all Seasons

Do you recall those magic days of spring,
when our love was young, and fresh and new,
and every bird could oh, so sweetly sing,
and every scented rose was touched with dew.

And passion in some secret place
beneath the twinkling stars of early summer,
the joy and warmth of your embrace
with winter's chill a far, far distant drummer.

You walked with me an autumn mellow measure,
between the fond remembered grassy hills,
each kiss the memory of a greater pleasure,
each glance, each touch, a harbinger of thrills.

While winter's breath has clothed the hills in rime,
I sit contented here, beside the hearth,
enough it is to feel your and in mine,
and know, my love, we trod a golden path.

H G Allen

To Thomas . . .

It seemed to me I'd never find
Someone who I could trust;
I kept my sadness deep inside
Because I thought I must.

No-one seemed to understand
I thought my fate was sealed;
They didn't know the hurt I bore -
A wound that never healed.

You came along and changed all that
I only wish you knew;
I have no pain and sadness now -
Because of love for you.

Kirsty Holland

Love in a Weather House

When I am out, she goes in and when she's in I'm out,
the situation's very sad of that I'm in no doubt.

I caught a glimpse of her yesterday, she waved I gave a smile,
it's looking a little cloudy, I might see her in a while.

It's hard living in a Weather House, for young folk 'specially so.
But we couldn't get a mortgage and have nowhere else to go.

No worries about safe sex, we never get that near.
For us it's global warming that holds the greatest fear.

If the weather never changes, I'll be stuck in all the time,
I'll be in and she'll be out until we're past our prime.

But they say the recession's bottomed out, we may leave and
go to town,
and then begin our married life in three up and two down.

Pauline Brennan

Second Honeymoon

And still within that Peak terrain,
Those golden days of love sublime,
I dreamed it happened all again -

A market town, a lord's domain,
The Derwent's bank, its steep incline;
And still within that same terrain

I saw you Robin's Stride attain
And on its pleateau'd top recline;
I dreamed it happened all again -

We wandered dale and winding lane
Beneath a brazen sun benign;
And still within that same terrain

I saw you by the Blue John vein,
Blonde hair a-glint in half-lit mine -
I dreamed it happened all again;

But more than all beside me lain
When we ourselves in love entwine -
And still within that Peak terrain
I dreamed it happened all again.

W Roy Harvey

Shadows of Shame

I played Romeo with your heart
Pledged, we'd never be apart
Sold you dreams, which you bought
Promises, promises without thought
How could I do such things to you
That shamefully, I confess, are all so true
How do you say sorry to a mistake
Knowing its already, far to late
The one wish, I'd ask -
If only I could, to put right that past
Regretfully you see, you gave so much to me
And knowing you still loved me when you died
Will always, break me up inside
The world title must be mine
For the biggest fool of all time
Sorry, but there's no excuse
To the amount, of that love abuse
Only tears of guilt, on my pitiful face
As I walk in shadows of disgrace.

Terry Sewell

Love Eternal Change Thou Not

I ask myself now what is love
The ethereal force of life renewed
Or are such feelings far above
Man's aspirations, aching fuelled?
Perhaps loves just like feeling good
A sense of joy, a flowered filled thing
With confused thoughts, I understood
That happiness, love's meant to bring.
For some love's just like a film
That threaded through projector runs
And man meets girl just on a whim
To stay with her 'til feelings turn.
Yet love, real love is strong, not thin
And stays and stays the years among.
Then tread the steady path alone
From cool beginning love may grow.
And, as I view it from our scene
Deny not that I love you so.
Stay, stay my love, you're all I know.

Cyril Saunders

Italian Relish

Poets through the ages have sung about your charms
filling many pages on the whiteness of your arms.
Swan-like neck and bosom fair;
textured fleck in glorious hair;
eyes of mystery, pools of light;
lips of cherry, teeth so bright -
Lady, small and shapely, don't you think it rather rum
that no one else has bothered to write about your bum?

Bill Shorto

Love

To lay entwined in a soft velvet dream
Held mesmerised in the gentle arms of love
Blended as one in a passionate embrace
Only aware of each others sweet desires.

Locked together in soul soothing rapture
Feeling the warm glow of two hearts on fire
Drinking on the honeyed wine of enchantment
Afloat on a green magic sea of tranquillity.

Seeing only silken love reflected in eager eyes
Hearing the sweet harmony of music in a kiss
Reaching over the heights of passions boundaries
content in the achievement of ecstatic satisfaction.

Dennis Best

Sunset

Nervously, holding me at the first,
Your urgency slowly strengthening.
What powerful yearnings my heart nursed
And longing love words your lips versed,
At the long day's shadows lengthening.

Tenderly, kissing me at the first,
Your soft mouth moistly parting
And my body, with a weakness, cursed
My eager wanting, unrehearsed,
At the martins' evening darting.

Passionately, taking me at the first,
Your strong hands keen demanding
And we, in love's oneness, immersed.
Our beginning and long days disperse
At Heaven's inexorable commanding.

J A Bradley

Untitled

Seldom have I realised, the definition
or sensation of love
for no words have yet, nor will ever
be created
to describe the warmth
that fills my heart
whilst I embrace you in my arms
yet this must surely be
the closest I will know

Steffan A Delon

Straight From the Heart

Love is like the sunshine
It makes your life so bright
Keeps you always happy
Be it day or night

Love is like the ocean
Like your heart so big and wide
When you've got a loved one
To whom you can confide

Love is like a rainbow
Colours glisten in your eyes
You see thing in perspective
Makes you good and wise

Love is like a fire
It can burn out of control
But it keeps you safe and warm
And can melt the hardest soul.

Love is just so perfect
Without it where would we be
Because the love I feel for you
Is the most important thing to me

Dawn Champion

A True Romantic

Do you leave love messages on her pillow
Send roses to show that you care,
Arrange weekends away in the country
And think of her everywhere?
Do you have candlelit dinners for two
And dance slowly to your favourite song,
Make her feel she's really special
'Cause in your eyes she can do no wrong?
Do you send passionate letters when parted
And ring her whenever you can,
Is she with you each night in your dreams
On moonlit walks on the sands?
Do you think about your future together
Is she there by your side as your wife,
'Cause you love her as you've loved no other
It's the greatest romance of your life.

Jackie Stallabrass

What is Love?

Love's a thing we all must hold
It's what we learn not what we're told
To share our love is to share our life.
That's why a man doth take a wife.

For then our lives begin to mould
For times when we are growing old.
So when you find the one you love
Treat her like a gentle dove.

You'll settle down one day no doubt
And wonder what loves all about
Trust each other and share your ways
And love will bloom throughout your days.

And when the children come along
Rejoice and sing a merry song
And think of those who have no child
For they are still so meek and mild.

Hugh Amott

First Love

When you notice the trees look much greener than green
And the sky's become bluer than you've ever seen.
When most things which annoy, now seem right though still wrong
And your heart is so light you could burst in to song.
This feeling within which you cannot explain
Puts your mind in such turmoil, even though you're still sane.
It's like butterflies wings gently fluttering inside.
And in each other only there's things you'll confide.
Secret moments to treasure 'til your very last day.
When you first fall in love, and both feel the same way.

Pamela Pitts

True Love

O what is love this many splendoured thing
That fills the heart and makes the spirit sing
A love so meek yet it can both unite
A love so strong that it can put to flight
All power that man does so perceive
And true love doth its won reward receive

A mother's love the dearest and the best
That has through countless ages stood the test
As women holds the infant to her breast

A love when lad sees lass and doth admire
It fills his heart with longing and desire
And love's first kiss so tender and so sweet
With loving eyes the boy does so entreat
The lass to love him only through the years
But when that love has gone brings on the tears

And boy grows into man along the way
With thoughts that true love comes to him one day
Or yet a secret love that only he
Can love her from afar and know that she
Cannot return that love for love is blind
And love comes from the heart and not the mind

The greatest love of all was that of He
Who died upon the Cross at Calvary.

William Arthur Littleford

My Lady

I have no gold or silver,
or gifts of any kind;
so fairest lady please accept,
rich treasures of my mind.

Soft pearls of thought,
and rubies; red as love
God's dew sent down; love's symbol
a pure white; milk white dove

Your beauty fired the arrow,
which pierced a lover's heart:
I send love's arrow back to you,
now love; your love impart.

Edward Holmes

Too Many Times

Too many *times* in my life*time*, I have longed for your return,
time after *time* I've remembered, the *time* for which I yearn.
The summer*time*, that happy *time*, when *time* just seems to fly,
I've longed to live that *time* again, some*time* before I die.
In *time* of war when *time*s were hard, it came my *time* to go.
Through winter*time* I thought of you, and *time* went by so slow.

Even in the summer*time,* the night-time seemed to drag,
Then came the *time* to go on leave, it was *time* to pack my bag.
I checked up in the *time*table, to find the *time*s of trains.
I left in good *time,* for the station, and walked through country lanes.
I heard the church clock strike the *time*, and found my watch was slow.
What a *time* to pour with rain, and still a mile to go.

As I broke into double *time*, the narrow track turned into slime.
I skidded about, and fell in the mud, *time*, after *time*, after *time.*
I reached the station just in *time,* to see the train disappear.
That *time* was the first *time* it left on *time,* since that *time* the previous year.
That left me with *time* to think of the *time*s, I've spent happy *time*s with you.
That *time* I had got *time* to burn, until the *time* the next was due.

Now the *time* has come, to see how *time* has changed your face,
I'm sad to say, that all that *time*, was of *time* of a total waste.

Ray Baker

Love

Where does love go when its ended,
Where does love go when it dies,
Back to the heart, where it came from,
Or does it end up as tears in the eyes.

What is this wondrous emotion,
Why is it born, if only to die,
And when it leaves you, what stays inside,
To make your heart break, and bring tears to your eyes,

How can we hold on to this treasure,
To retain it and keep in our hearts,
It's wondrous when new, illusive it's true,
It can shatter our whole word apart.

It is madness to love so completely,
You can never be sure it will last,
It is heady, like wine, completely divine,
But what when the magic has passed.

There is always tomorrow remember,
Forget all the heartache and pain,
You must go on constantly searching,
Until you find love again.

Edna Watford Harvey

Love After Marriage

You love me despite my faults,
Of course I've more than you,
Not that you would ever say
What obviously is true!

My diets never last more
Than a day or two,
You love me plump
Is all I hear from you.

I've been tempted, during married years,
By men of position or wealth
But you've never wavered dear
Just loved me for myself.

I love you darling, can't you tell,
We have a passion strong,
No-one can break what ties us,
I'm here where I belong.

Winifred Putt

Judith

If a gentle summer breeze
Could soothe away, the pains
Of a lifetime of giving,
I wish you an endless summer.

If all your faded hopes and dreams
Could bloom and flower anew,
I wish you the blessed
April rain.

If my every loving thought
Were voiced in a skylark's note,
I would have him sing for you
Eternally.

Alfred Dewsbury

A Parisian Tale

If you are in love, you should go to Paris in the spring,
My friends said.
We went in autumn.

The city is beautiful and the Parisians glow,
I was told.
Only one was true.

Crushed in the Metro, lost in the streets, booked
Into crumbling hotels.
Nothing was right.

Except that you and I were together,
Fighting and loving,
In terrible, wonderful Paris.

J M Hall

A Garden

The offer of a house to rent,
In a country town in rural Kent,
A heartfelt, 'Thankyou,' our reply,
A dream come true for Charles and I.
We loved the house, with room for guest,
But even more, our interest.
The garden bounded by a hedge,
With space for flowers, fruit and veg;
April was our time of moving,
Sun and rain the earth improving
With what zest we dug and planted,
Or relaxed there, quite enchanted.
Six years of pleasure, joy and pride,
Passed quickly, then my dear Charles died,
Despairing, stunned and without hope,
Friends and the garden helped me cope.
April returned with sun and gale,
The house was then put up for sale,
And I must move to pastures new,
Please let there be a garden too.

A M Le Petit

Searching - a Daydream

I'm looking for a lover - a man who doesn't snore,
A guy who's thoughtful and romantic too.
I'm looking for a lover, not an overwhelming bore,
Just a man who loves me - nothing more.

I'm looking for a lover, a fella I'd adore,
To feed and cherish daily - wouldn't you?
I'm looking for a lover, as you've heard me say before,
Please Fate, lend me a hand, I do implore.

Now, should I find my lover, this man who doesn't snore
We'll have a life of bliss - it's true, I'm sure.
I'm looking for a lover who's not over sixty-four.
Are you out there - the man I'm looking for?

Beth Roman

To My Love

Stirring at three am (you slept),
I felt your hand congenial upon my hip.
I lay still, touch-tied.
Warmer than wool, the gesture
Entered my dreams, the texture
Of your palm snugger than blankets.

Sylvia Dewhirst

Magic Dust

If I had some magic dust
I'd sprinkle it around
I'd sprinkle it just every where
And cover all the ground.

It would fill the air with love
And with special care
I'd sprinkle it in every place
Where trouble often dominates.

And where there's suffering and pain
It would make them well again
I'd sprinkle it so generously
On every nation and country.

I'd sprinkle it on people too
Who suffer stress and strain
With all the worry and sadness
Our hearts would sing again.

In every corner of the earth
The dust would settle there
A peaceful happy world for all
For every country large or small.

Edna Thompson

Unrequited Love

For long, long years I loved you
And asked nothing in return
But to feel your arms around me
At times to ease the pain
But you didn't know what love is
And left without a sound.

Not a backward glance
Not a look around
To see what you'd left behind
Now the days are long
And nights draw on
Just empty sighs
Now that you've gone.

But as you grow older
As I am now
You'll think and sigh
Like I
And wish you'd thought again.

I know you're unhappy
And cry in pain
Don't you wish
To turn back the clock
Again.

Roy Whitfield

Please . . .

I want to feel your arms enfold me
Hear sweet words that no-one's told me,
To see you, hear you, touch you, smell
The manliness I know, so well.
These things meant for the lucky only
While Joycey stands alone and lonely,
To work all week to earn my money
And never reap rewards . . . not funny,
I come home to an empty place
And knowing, sometimes I can't face
The quiet room, the vacant chair
The feeling that there's no-one there,
Please think of me when work is done
For Joycey's missing all the fun,
Why tease me with your tender touch
You know that I want you, so much,
Why hold me, thrill me, with your kiss
There must be more to life than this,
Please . . . tell me, show me, that you care
And let me, please . . . that moment share . . .

Joyce Tryhorn

Love

Faith and hope and charity
Are virtues from above
But the greatest of them all
Is the priceless gift of love.

True love is never shallow
It's born deep within the heart
And it shows in kindly service
To those near and far apart.

Love can never be measured
In terms of material worth
And only a heart free from hate
Can ever bring it to birth.

The fire of love is consuming
Burning out hatred and sin
But leaving our lives open
To welcome our Saviour in.

Genevieve Tuke

Quiet Times

In the quiet time,
When darkness
Enveloped our faces,
I whispered,
'Do you love me?'
'Yes,
But not enough.'

A M Wasikowska

Alone With Love

You have left, yet I sense you near to me,
I feel our love so strong, will forever be.
I gaze at your picture, your happy smile, your dancing eyes are here.
I speak to you, grateful for the happy times - forgive the tear.
Should you see one fall, do not be sad.
We lived and loved each day, until the last you had.
I remember our romantic times, special just to us
Breakfast in New York, Venice on the water bus.
Strolling down a country lane, sunsets we'd admire.
Lake Garda in the mornings, listening to a choir.
Our special celebrations, you never once forgot.
The fun we shared and how you laughed a lot.
Wait for me dear until we meet once more
Our souls entwined as one, together, as before.
I take flowers to place upon your stone,
I leave you love - then - I walk away alone.

Caleta Thomas

For You

If someone should come along one day
Smile and say *Hello*
Then steal your heart away
How would you feel?

How would you feel
If he took you out one night
And you strolled in the moonlight,
Would you treat him right?

If he looked into your eyes
Reduced you to breathless sighs,
Would you love him forever?
Could you be so good together?

If he wrote you poetry
Then perhaps you would see
Perhaps that someone
Could be me.

Antony Haselton

Eternal Love

(For E - after 47 years)

Eternal love that far exceeds, outruns, the green
Desires and whims of callow youth,
Indelible, penned fast upon my proffered heart,
The stark epitome of loyalty and truth.
Here is no momentary fancy, passing lust, but
Moulded by dire hardships to withstand times test
And then, as this life ebbs, to journey on undying,
Refreshed, renewed in realms beyond the furthest stars,
You were my love, you are my love, let heaven tell the rest!

Stan Clayton

If I Couldn't Think of You

This world would be a dismal place
Each passing day would be so long
If I couldn't call to mind your face
Or sing our favourite song.

If I couldn't think about your kiss
Or dream of passion so devine
Or anticipate of future bliss
When you are really mine.

If I couldn't gaze up to the sun
And see your smile reflecting there
Or in solitude when day is done
To feel in thoughts you're always near.

If I couldn't see in autumn rain
The shameless tears we two have shed
Or when walking down a country lane
The mingled footprints where we tread.

This world would be a dismal place
Each passing day would be so blue
And life would be so hard to face
If I couldn't think of you!

Elizabeth Davey

Only in Dreams

Only in dreams, my love, only in dreams
I run to you and clasp you to my heart.
More real to me than life that dream-world seems,
Before the prying dawn thrusts us apart.
Only in sleep, my love, only in sleep
My longing arms encircle your dear form.
The jealous daylight will not let me keep
Your treasured smile, your kisses sweet and warm.
Only at night, my love, only at night
I dare to dream of joys that may not be.
Too soon the cock's shrill call awakes the light
That bears you, darling girl, away from me.
Your image fades, my love, but oh, the bliss
Of that last fond embrace; that last sweet kiss.

John Clark

The Haymaker's Passion

John was pitching the hay,
When a lady went his way,
Her beautiful blue eyes,
Took him by surprise,
On a fine summer's day.

Oh, her floating hair,
Those features so fair,
When she sat in his cart,
And stole his heart,
With her graceful air.

The sweet song from her lips,
And those elegant hips,
And the way she dressed,
With that heaving breast,
Was so hard to resist.

Come my love, let us lay,
In the bed of hay,
But she broke his embrace,
With a slap on his face,
And went upon her way.

A R Leonard

Overkill

The Colonel's daughter has a wedding day
With ceremonial her heart desires.
Important people in the parish church,
Older, but tolerant of young passion's fires.

The Bridegroom, polished to the last degree
Despite his humble rank; stiff upper lip
And hands that tremble yet for all to see,
Ignores the Best Man's reassuring grip.

An archway of young Officers, of course,
With upheld sword-blades glinting in the sun;
Then photographs, champagne and revelry,
Relaxing now, with formal duty done.

It could have been a sadly different tale.
Her father's high position she must thank.
A white-beribboned shotgun you'd expect . . . but
Wherever did he get the Chieftain tank?

Audrey Forbes-Handley

The Song of the World

My love,
Now she lies with me . . . warm, in sleep.
As sleep lies well upon our eyes.
Their beauty in dreams I recall,
In the season of the fall.
As the world turns,
The flame of all desire burns.
And from this flame -
The song of the world we name.

Francis Paul Farnworth

The Gift

Love is a quality,
Fruit of Infinity,
A gem beyond compare
Which all the kingdoms share.
The ultimate cosmic grace,
Unconfined by time or space.
Throbbing pulses faster beat
When the lips of lovers meet.
Love is music in the air
With cadences so fair.
Thro' the veil we see,
The apple on the tree,
See compassion, sacrifice,
Love's the leaven of life.
It casts a nimbus bright
On all who seek the light.

Anna Punshon

Hope or Despair

What must I do to win his love - assure him mine is true
Walk backwards up Mount Everest and shout, 'That was for you?'

He dreams of love as white-hot fire but someday perhaps he'll learn
That ere flames turn to ashes they can very cruelly burn
Desire without foundation drifts away like shifting sand
While love that grows from friendship like a rock can firmly stand.

Himself not last spring's hatching, he must surely face the truth
And then won't care and sympathy make up for utmost youth?
With patient, gentle humour all his faults to tolerate
Can't warmth and understanding for mere beauty compensate?
Aren't vintage wines more mellow and aren't riper fruits more sweet
And, long term, isn't temperate sun more kind than tropic heat?

So how can I convince him what I know deep in my heart?
That somehow we'd have better lives together than apart!

Mandy Smith

Hand in Hand

We're walking together,
Just hand in hand.
For the love of you,
I'd take any stand.
In our love for each other,
We are equal.
There is no demand.
We're walking together,
Just hand in hand.
My heart is singing,
It's beat is a powerful band.
Both of us don't claim perfection,
But our love for each other,
Grows in the right direction.
Your voice is a love potion,
You are my true devotion.
Our love is causing a commotion.
Your hand squeezes mine,
Our love is always,
For all time . . .

David Wesley Cooper